In the Name
of Honor

IN THE NAME OF HONOR

A MEMOIR

Mukhtar Mai

With Marie-Thérèse Cuny
translated by Linda Coverdale

Foreword by Nicholas D. Kristof

Washington Square Press
New York London Toronto Sydney

Washington Square Press
A Division of Simon & Schuster, Inc.
1230 Avenue of the Americas
New York, NY 10020

Published by arrangement with Oh! Editions, Paris
Originally published as *Déshonorée* in France in 2006 by Oh! Editions, Paris

All photographs appearing in the insert are courtesy of Philippe Robinet and
Marie-Thérèse Cuny

First Washington Square Press trade paperback edition October 2007

WASHINGTON SQUARE PRESS and colophon are registered trademarks
of Simon & Schuster, Inc.

For information about special discounts for bulk purchases, please contact
Simon & Schuster Special Sales at 1-800-456-6798 or
business@simonandschuster.com.

Manufactured in the United States of America

10 9 8 7 6 5 4 3 2

ISBN-13: 978-1-4165-3228-6
ISBN-10:   1-4165-3228-5
ISBN-13: 978-1-4165-3229-3 (pbk)
ISBN-10:   1-4165-3229-3 (pbk)

A Note to the Reader

Mukhtar Mai is a thirty-three-year-old Pakistani peasant woman. She lives in Meerwala, a small village in southern Punjab, near the border with India.

When journalists reported that she had been condemned by her village tribal council to be gang-raped, the horrifying news made headlines around the world. Although illiterate and apparently powerless, Mukhtar Mai was courageous, and she became the first woman in her country to reclaim her honor by fighting back against a barbarous tradition that almost destroyed her.

My colleagues and I made the arduous journey to the remote village of Meerwala, where we were welcomed by Mukhtar Mai and her friend Naseem Akhtar. They were amazed that we had come all the way from France to suggest to Mukhtar Mai that we should write a book together, a book that would help her in her struggle. After several hours of discussion, we all agreed that her book would be published in France, and that she would come to Paris to help launch it.

Marie-Thérèse Cuny, a writer who has long dedicated herself to the cause of women's rights, arrived in Meerwala a few weeks later. Mukhtar Mai speaks only Saraiki and can read or write no other language. Mustafa Baloch and Saif Khan therefore facilitated the collaboration between the two women by translating their conversations. Marie-Thérèse Cuny transformed Mukhtar's emotions, thoughts, and impressions into this book, despite the hurdle posed by the great disparity of language.

Linda Coverdale's translation from French to English was an attempt to faithfully reproduce Mukhtar Mai's story as reported in the French edition.

In January 2006, after being received along with our entire editorial staff by the French minister of foreign affairs, Mukhtar Mai spoke about women's rights on the Place des Droits de l'Homme, which is dedicated to the rights of all mankind.

Philippe Robinet
Publisher
Oh! Editions, France

Foreword

I don't know whether people felt this when they were around Mother Teresa or Martin Luther King Jr., but around Mukhtar Mai I can feel true greatness. Her village of Meerwala is an unassuming collection of huts, and she can be shy and quiet, but you follow her through the village and you sense that she is leading a revolution—against rape, illiteracy, and the repression of women—that is reverberating through all of Pakistan and indeed the entire world.

The backdrop of Mukhtar's story is well-known: Her young brother was accused (wrongly) of having an affair, and so a tribal council decided to punish her family by ordering that she be gang-raped. The sentence was carried out then and there, and she was forced to walk home nearly naked before a jeering crowd. She was meant to commit suicide, and initially she thought she would—but then she became more angry than humiliated. Instead of killing herself, she prosecuted her attackers and told her story.

If Mukhtar's story had ended there, it would have been one more tragedy in a world full of them. Fortunately, that was just the beginning, for Mukhtar used her compensation money from the rape to start a school in her village. Ultimately, she believed that the only way to fight feudal attitudes was to educate people.

I had heard of Mukhtar's story, and in 2004 while on a visit to Pakistan I traveled to Meerwala to meet her. (Back then she mostly went by a variant of her name, Mukhtaran Bibi.) Visiting her involved a succession of flights from Islamabad to Lahore to Multan, and then a drive for several hours through the Punjab countryside, ending up on a dirt road. Meerwala then had no electricity, and when I finally got to her house her father and brothers were introduced to me but she hung back. If I had expected a magnetic and charismatic leader, that wasn't her—she struck me instead as retiring and a bit traditional. She didn't seem to think it was appropriate for a woman to do much talking, and so at first her brothers and father spoke.

Gradually, though, she began speaking to me more. She spoke bluntly of her shame at being raped, of crying endlessly, of having disgraced her family. She spoke passionately about her school, and increasingly she dominated the room. Mukhtar told me that her school was running out of money, so she was selling family jewelry to pay the teachers; she was at her wit's end. The police who were supposedly protecting her were losing interest, and she feared she would soon be killed. After our interview, she took me aside and pretty much begged me to help—with a force that belied my initial impression of a wallflower.

I wrote a column about Mukhtar and the responses deluged my office. American readers were moved by her story and wanted to help. I blithely told readers they could send checks, and I would forward them to her. Eventually, I was able to arrange to do so through the aid group Mercy Corps, and in the end readers sent more than $160,000, which she used to buy a van to function as an ambulance and school bus, and to start a high school.

Since that first trip, I've seen Mukhtar repeatedly—both in New York and in Meerwala. In the U.S. she appears at banquets, is hailed at the White House, and is feted at luxury hotels—and yet she is always counting the days to return to Pakistan. At one banquet for the elite of New York, she had Pakistani food brought to her. She also takes in the sights of New York with aplomb. I thought she would be scandalized by America, but she didn't even blush when she opened up the *Glamour* magazine that featured an article about her (including photos of her that set a record for clothing-to-skin ratio for any fashion magazine). She continues to cover her hair in New York, and she is a proud—but not judgmental—Pakistani wherever she goes.

For all the acclaim and goodwill that Mukhtar has won for Pakistan, she has had mostly trouble from Pakistan's leaders. I think the problem is twofold. First, they feel she is displaying Pakistan's dirty laundry in public, embarrassing her country. Second, they're resentful that an uneducated peasant woman from a Punjab village is celebrated as a hero, getting more attention than they are. The upshot is the government has repeatedly tried to muzzle her.

One early instance came when Mukhtar was planning to come to the U.S. for a conference. President Musharraf personally ordered that she be put on the "exit control list" to stop her from leaving the country, and the authorities took her passport. When she complained publicly to me about this, the authorities in effect kidnapped her and took her to Islamabad. But she continued to speak out, and ultimately the incident was a huge embarrassment for President Musharraf— and Mukhtar emerged more prominent than ever.

Most troubling of all is that one of President Musharraf's closest friends, Brigadier Ijaz Shah, traveled to Lahore in 2005 to deliver a threat to Amna Buttar, a Pakistani-American physician in Wisconsin who runs a human rights organization (www.4anaa.org) and who has strongly supported Mukhtar. Amna routinely travels with Mukhtar on American visits, interprets for her, and has generally played a heroic role in pushing for the rights of women in Pakistan. The Brigadier warned Amna that she and Mukhtar should be careful and not stir up trouble, and he added that Pakistani intelligence knows about everything they do. Alluding to a planned visit by Mukhtar and Amna to

New York, he added: "We can do anything. We can just pay a little money to some black guys in New York and get people killed there."

That was not only racist, but also a blunt threat to kill Amna and Mukhtar on American soil. When I asked the Pakistani government about the threat, Shah sent me a statement acknowledging that he had met with Amna but denied making any threat.

Late in 2005, Mukhtar was planning to speak at the U.N. It had all been arranged for weeks, and she dropped by my office just before going to give her speech. The organizers called my office, frantically looking for her: the speech had been canceled, on orders of the Pakistani government. Once more, the Pakistani leaders had shot themselves in the foot: few Americans would have known of Mukhtar's speech had it gone ahead, but now it became a well-known incident.

In Pakistan as well, the government has applied constant pressure on Mukhtar. Her mail is confiscated, her phones are tapped. Newspapers close to the government constantly publish disparaging articles about her, suggesting that she is living it up abroad or that she is an unpatriotic woman who allows herself to be used by foreigners and agents for India (like myself) to make Pakistan look bad.

Mukhtar is sensitive, and these criticisms really sting her. But over time, I've watched her mature and toughen. When I first visited her, she was still asking her brothers for permission every time she wanted to leave the house. That became ridiculous as she began to jet around the world and be feted by foreign ministers, so Mukhtar just breached tradition and came and went as she saw fit—but her brothers disapproved. She and her brothers love each other, of course, but there is a fundamental tension about what a woman should do on her own, and that is hard on all of them.

In March 2006 I visited Meerwala again, and I was impressed by Mukhtar's schools. They are much better equipped today, and now the English teachers can actually speak English. The high school was under construction, and at the elementary school graduation there was a wonderful school play in which the kids acted out the dangers of early marriage (the main danger turned out to be that the wife is murdered). But what struck me the most in Meerwala was how

Mukhtar tirelessly browbeat parents to keep their daughters in school. The parents of one little fourth grader named Sidra had planned to pull her out of school to marry her off, for example, so Mukhtar bullied them into dropping those plans and keeping the girl in school. Now Sidra wants to be a doctor.

That is why Mukhtar keeps refusing to move to safety in the city, or even to a haven in the West. Life might be more comfortable, but she would lose that sense of fulfillment that she now finds. This is a woman on a mission.

Most poignant of all is the scene in Mukhtar's home. Desperate women from across Pakistan arrive in buses and taxis and carts, for they have heard of Mukhtar and hope that she may help. The worst cases have had their noses cut off—a common Pakistani punishment administered to women in order to shame them forever. So Mukhtar hears them out and tries to arrange doctors or lawyers or other help for them. In the meantime these women sleep with Mukhtar on the floor of her bedroom (she gave the bed to the principal of her elementary school, Naseem Akhtar). So every night, there are up to a dozen women sleeping with Mukhtar in her bedroom, lying all over the floor, huddled against one another, comforting one another. They are victims with wrenching stories—and yet they are also symbols of hope, signs that times are changing and that women are fighting back.

Women who were raped simply killed themselves, but increasingly they are following Mukhtar's example. Other victims, like Dr. Shazia Khalid, have become anti-rape activists in their own right, but Dr. Shazia is quick to acknowledge that she found the courage to stand up only because Mukhtar had paved the way. The increased likelihood that a rape victim will refuse to commit suicide and will instead seek to prosecute her attackers is in turn creating a real disincentive for rape, and so the number of rapes seems to be dropping in the area around Meerwala. Gradually, Mukhtar is chipping away at the old repressive way of life, and helping to usher in a new Pakistan.

As you read *In the Name of Honor,* I think you will find a story that is tremendously inspiring rather than one that tells of brutality and despair. By the alchemy of her courage and stubbornness, Mukhtar has taken a sordid tale of gang rape and turned it into something heartwarming and hopeful. And that is one more reason why, when I'm around Mukhtar, I sense that this shy peasant woman is truly a great and historic figure—and why she's one of my heroes.

Nicholas D. Kristof

The Long Road Ahead

On the night of June 22, 2002, our family reaches a decision.

I, Mukhtaran Bibi, a woman of the peasant Gujar caste, living in the village of Meerwala, will be the one to confront an influential and aggressive local clan, farmers of the powerful Mastoi caste, on behalf of my family.

My little brother Shakur is accused by the Mastois of having "spoken" to Salma, a young woman of their clan. Shakur is only twelve years old, while Salma is over twenty. We know my brother has done nothing wrong, but if the Mastois have decided otherwise, we Gujars must bow to their demands. This is the way it has always been.

My father and uncle have explained the situation to me.

"Our mullah, Abdul Razzaq, is in despair. The Mastois have the majority in the village council, and they refuse all reconciliation. They are armed. Your maternal uncle and Ramzan Pachar, a friend of the Mastois, have tried everything to calm the members of the council. We have but one last chance: a Gujar woman must appear before their clan. Among all the women of our house, we have chosen you."

"Why me?"

"The others are too young to do this. Your husband has granted you a divorce, you have no children, you teach the Koran. You are a respectable woman!"

It's long after sunset, but until now I've been told very little of what caused this serious dispute today. The men of the jirga, our village council, have been meeting for several hours now, and only they know why I must appear before that tribunal.

Shakur has been missing since midday. All we know is that at noon he was in a wheat field near our house, but tonight he is locked up inside the police station, three miles from the village. I hear from my own father's lips that my little brother has been beaten.

"We saw Shakur when the police brought him out

of the Mastois' house. He was all bloody, and his clothes were torn. The police took him away in handcuffs without letting me speak to him. I'd been looking for him everywhere, and a man who'd been cutting branches up in a palm tree came to tell me that he'd seen the Mastois kidnap Shakur. In the village, people began reporting to me that the Mastois were accusing him of illicit conduct and theft."

The Mastois are old hands at this kind of retaliation. Their powerful clan leader knows many influential people, and they are violent men, capable of invading anyone's home with their guns to loot, rape, and tear the place apart. The lower-caste Gujars have no right to oppose them, and no one in my family has dared go to their house.

Because of his religious office, the mullah is the only person entitled to intervene in this crisis, but all his efforts have been in vain. So my father went to file a complaint with the police. Outraged that a Gujar peasant has defied them by sending policemen to their very doorstep, the proud Mastois have slightly modified their story: now they accuse Shakur of raping Salma. They claim that my brother has committed *zina-bil-jabar*, which in Pakistan means the sins of rape, adultery, or sexual relations without the sanctity of marriage. Before handing over my brother, the Mastois demanded that he be locked up, and they insisted that if he were released from jail, he should be returned to the custody of the Mastoi clan. *Zina* may be punishable by death, according to the Islamic code of sharia, so the police have locked up Shakur not only because he is accused of a serious crime but also to protect him from the violent Mastois, who want to take justice into their own hands. The whole village has known about all this since early this afternoon, and my father has taken the women of my family to our neighbors' houses for safety's sake. We know that the Mastois always take their revenge on a woman of a lower caste. It's the woman's place to humiliate herself, to beg for forgiveness before all the men of the village assembled in a jirga in front of the Mastois' farmhouse.

That farm is barely three hundred yards from ours, yet I know it only by sight: imposing walls, and a terrace from which they look out over the neighborhood as though they were the lords of the earth.

• • •

"Mukhtaran, get ready, and follow us."

That night, I have no idea that the path leading from our little farm to the wealthier home of the Mastois will change my life forever. If the men of the Mastoi clan accept my apologies, the path will be short. Although my mission is a dangerous one, I am confident. I set out, clasping the Koran to my breast. The Koran will protect me.

My father made the only possible choice. I am twenty-eight, and I may not know how to read or write, since there is no school for girls in our village, but I have learned the Koran by heart, and ever since my divorce I have taught its verses to our local children as an act of charity. That is my respectability. And my strength.

I walk along the dirt path, followed by my father, my uncle Haji Altaf, and Ghulamnabi, a friend of another caste, who has been acting as an intermediary during the negotiations of the jirga. They are afraid for my safety, and my uncle even hesitated himself before coming with me. Yet I proceed along the path with a kind of childlike trust. I have committed no crime. I have not personally done anything wrong. I believe in God, and since my divorce I have been living dutifully in peaceful seclusion with my family, far from the world of men. No one has ever spoken ill of me, as often happens with other women. Salma, for example, is known for her bold ways: that girl has a saucy tongue, and she gets around. She goes out when and where she pleases. It's possible that the Mastois have tried to take advantage of my young brother's innocence to cover up something involving Salma. Be that as it may, the Mastois decide, and the Gujars obey.

The June night still burns with the heat of the day; the birds are asleep, and the goats, too. Somewhere a dog barks in the silence surrounding my footsteps, a silence that grows into a faint rumbling. As I walk on, I begin to hear the voices of angry men, whom I can now see illuminated by the single light at the entrance to the Mastois' farm. There are more than a hundred men gathered near the mosque, perhaps as many as two hundred to two hundred and fifty, and most of them are Mastois. They are the ones dominating the jirga. Although he is our village mullah, even Abdul Razzaq cannot oppose them. I look for him in the crowd; he is not there. I am unaware at the time that after disagreeing with the Mastois over how to handle the affair, certain members of the jirga have left the council. The Mastois are now in charge.

Before me I see Faiz Mohammed along with four men: Abdul Khaliq, Ghulam Farid, Allah Dita, and Mohammed Faiz. They are armed with rifles and a pistol, which they point immediately at the men of my clan. The Mastois wave their guns around to frighten off my family, but my father and uncle don't budge. Held at bay by Faiz, they stand at my back.

The Mastois have gathered their clan behind them, a threatening wall of impatient and agitated men.

I have brought a shawl, which I spread out at their feet as a sign of allegiance. From memory, I recite a verse from the Koran, holding my hand on the holy book. Everything I know of the scriptures I have learned by listening, not reading, but I may well be more familiar with the sacred texts than are most of these brutes who stare at me contemptuously. The moment has come for the honor of the Mastois to be made pure once again. The Punjab, which is known as The Land of Five Rivers, is also called The Land of the Pure. But who are the pure ones?

The Mastois unnerve me with their guns and evil faces—especially Abdul Khaliq and his pistol. He has the eyes of a madman, glaring with hatred. But although I certainly know my place as a member of an inferior caste, I also have a sense of honor, the honor of the Gujars. Our community of small, impoverished farmers has been here for several hundred years, and while I'm not familiar with our history in detail, I feel that it is part of me, in my blood. I stand there trembling, with downcast eyes.

I venture to look up, but Faiz says nothing, shaking his head in disdain. For a few moments, all is quiet. I pray silently, and then fear strikes, abruptly, like a monsoon deluge, numbing my body with a lightning bolt.

Now I can see in the eyes of that man that he wanted a Gujar woman to appear before the Mastois' jirga so that he could take revenge on her in front of the entire village. These men have fooled the mullah, my father, my entire family, and the councilors of the jirga to which they themselves belong. This is the first time that the councilors themselves have fixed upon a gang rape as a means to what they call their "honor justice."

Abdul Khaliq turns to his kinsmen, who are as eager as he is to carry out that verdict, to demonstrate their power through a show of force. Abdul Khaliq then grabs my arm, while Ghulam Farid, Allah Dita, and Mohammed Faiz start pushing me.

I am there, true, but it isn't me anymore: this petrified body, these collapsing legs no longer belong to me. I am about to faint, to fall to the ground, but I never get the chance—they drag me away like a goat led to slaughter. Men's arms have seized mine, pulling at my clothes, my shawl, my hair.

"In the name of the Koran, release me!" I scream. "In the name of God, let me go!"

I pass from one night to another, taken from the darkness outside to the darkness inside an enclosed place where I can distinguish those four men only by the moonlight filtering through a tiny window. Four walls and a door, guarded by an armed silhouette.

Escape is impossible. Prayer is impossible.

That is where they rape me, on the beaten earth of

an empty stable. Four men: Abdul Khaliq, Gulam Farid, Allah Dita, and Mohammed Faiz. I don't know how long that vicious torture lasts. An hour? All night?

I, Mukhtaran Bibi, eldest daughter of my father, Ghulam Farid Jat, lose all consciousness of myself, but I will never forget the faces of those animals. For them, a woman is simply an object of possession, honor, or revenge. They marry or rape them according to their conception of tribal pride. They know that a woman humiliated in that way has no other recourse except suicide. They don't even need to use their weapons. Rape kills her. Rape is the ultimate weapon: it shames the other clan forever.

They don't bother to beat me. I am already at their mercy, they are threatening my relatives, and my brother is in jail. I am forced to submit.

Then they shove me outside, half naked, where I stumble and fall. They throw my shalwar at me. This time, the double wooden doors of the stable close on the four men. Everyone is waiting. I am alone with my shame before the eyes of the entire village. I have no words to describe what I am at that moment. I can't think: a dense fog has clouded my brain, masking the images of torture and infamous submission. I call out for my father, who tosses me his shawl to help me preserve the only dignity I have left. I walk without knowing where I'm going, heading instinctively toward my family's house. I drift like a ghost along that path, with my father, my uncle, and his friend Ramzan following me at a distance.

My mother is weeping outside our home. I walk past her, dazed, mute, accompanied in silence by other women. I enter one of the three rooms in the women's quarters and crumple onto a straw pallet, where I lie motionless under a blanket. My life has just collapsed into such horror that my mind and body will not accept reality. I had no idea such violence was possible. I was naive, used to living under the protection of a father and eldest brother, like all the women in my province.

Married at eighteen by my family to a man I did not know and who proved both lazy and incompetent, I had managed to obtain a divorce rather quickly, with the help of my father, and had been living sheltered from the outside world—a world that extended no farther than my native village. Illiterate, like all the other women around me, I led a life reduced to the usual housekeeping tasks and a few simple activities. I gave free instruction in the Koran to the village children, who learned the holy book as I had, by ear. And to contribute to our meager family earnings, I taught women what I knew best: embroidery. From sunrise to sunset, my existence was bounded by the land of my father's small farm and set to the rhythm of daily chores and seasonal harvests. Aside from what I had discovered during my marriage, which had placed me temporarily in another family's home, I knew nothing beyond the life led by all the women in my little world.

Fate has just torn me from that reassuring life, and I cannot understand why I am being punished. I feel, quite simply, dead. Unable to think. Unable to rise above this stunning suffering that overwhelms and paralyzes me.

All the women are weeping around me. I can feel hands stroking my head and my shoulders to comfort me. My younger sisters sob while I lie there without moving, strangely remote from the misfortune that has befallen me and affected my whole family. For three days, I leave that room only to relieve myself, but I never eat, or cry, or speak. I can hear my mother talking to me.

"You must forget, Mukhtaran. It's over. The police will let your brother go."

I hear other words too.

"Shakur committed an offense, he raped Salma!" claims a woman in the village.

"Mukhtaran should have married a Mastoi, as the mullah said, and Shakur should have wed Salma," insists another woman. "She's the one who refused. It's her own fault."

Words fly through the village like white pigeons or black crows, depending on who is speaking. Little by little, I begin to understand where these rumors have come from.

The negotiations held by the jirga, which normally meets in the home of Mullah Abdul Razzaq, were conducted in the street this time, in the middle of the village. This traditional tribal council operates without any official sanction, undertaking to resolve local disputes in ways that serve—in principle—the best interests of each party. In our villages, most peasants cannot afford to hire a lawyer, so people prefer to appeal to a jirga because the government's justice costs too much. As for the charge of rape brought against my brother, I don't understand why the jirga was unable to negotiate any settlement. Women are rarely informed about the decisions of men, and my father and uncle have told me very little, but thanks to the hearsay that reaches us from the village, I begin to realize why I have been punished.

Word has it that Shakur was caught flirting with Salma. Other rumors say he stole stalks of sugarcane from a field, which is what the Mastois had claimed at first, it seems. After accusing him of rape, the clan kidnapped, beat, and sodomized my brother to humiliate him. It was not until much later that Shakur spoke of these things, and then only to our father. He had tried several times to escape from the Mastois, but they had always recaptured him.

Then, to conceal the rape of my young brother from the jirga, the Mastois invented a new account in which Shakur had had sexual relations with Salma, who was supposedly a virgin. A dreadful crime. Girls are forbidden even to talk to boys. If a woman encounters a man, she must lower her eyes and never address him under any pretext.

When I see Shakur go through the courtyard, I just

cannot imagine any such "crime." He's only twelve or thirteen years old! (Where we live, a young person's age is known only from the lips of the mother or father: "This year, you are five years old . . ."—or ten, or twenty. We have no birth certificates, since a birth is not registered anywhere.) My skinny young brother is still a child and could not have had relations with any girl.

Salma is a rather wild young woman in her twenties. She may well have said something provocative to my brother, which is just like her, but he's certainly guilty of nothing more than encountering her at the edge of the Mastois' wheat field. Some in the village say that he flirted with her, or at least spoke to her, while others maintain that they were caught sitting together, holding hands. Depending on which clans these villagers belong to, the truth fades away in the dust of people's words. . . .

Shakur has done nothing wrong, I'm sure of it.

Only my own ordeal rivals what he confided to our father about the agonies he went through that day.

All these things whirl endlessly through my head for almost a week. Why him? And why me? That family simply wanted to destroy ours.

And I hear again that an initial proposal was supposedly made to the Mastois by Mullah Abdul Razzaq, when he said that the wise way to calm everyone down and avoid a permanent feud between the families was to give Shakur in marriage to Salma, and have the eldest Gujar daughter, myself, wed a Mastoi in exchange. Some people insist that I refused, and that I was therefore responsible for what happened to me, because I thwarted the reconciliation. Other council members, however, say that it was the Mastoi chieftain himself who rejected this misalliance.

"I'll break everything in their house!" he even screamed. "I'll slaughter the livestock and rape the women!"

That was when the mullah left the council, having no other proposition to offer. In the end it was Ramzan, the only one present who belonged neither to the Mastoi caste nor to ours, who convinced my father and uncle to try another tactic: asking for forgiveness. By sending a respectable woman of my age to show submission before those savages—submission that would persuade the Mastois to be merciful and withdraw their accusations, so that the police could free my brother. And that is why I set out confidently to confront those fiends without anyone imagining that I would fall victim to that last attempt at reconciliation.

After my rapists shoved me out of the stable, however, Shakur was not released, so that very night, one of my cousins went to see Faiz, the Mastoi chieftain.

"What you have done is done. Now, have Shakur set free."

"Go to the police station, I'll speak to them afterward."

My cousin went to the police station.

"I spoke to Faiz; he said to let the boy go."

The policeman telephoned Faiz, as though that man were his boss.

"Someone has just shown up here claiming that you agreed to have Shakur released. . . ."

"Let him pay to have the boy set free. Take the money, then let him go."

The police asked for twelve thousand rupees, an enormous sum for our family, the equivalent of three or four months' salary for a workman. My father and uncle made the rounds of all our cousins and neighbors to get the money together and went back that same night to give it to the police. My brother was finally released at around one o'clock in the morning and was brought back by my uncle and Ramzan Pachar.

But he is still in danger. The Mastois' hatred will never flag: they will pursue their accusation until the bitter end, because they cannot retreat without losing face and honor. And a Mastoi never gives in. They are there, in their house, the clan leader and his brothers, on the other side of the sugarcane field. Within sight. They have triumphed over my brother and me, but a war has been declared. The Mastois, who belong to a warrior caste, are all armed, while we have only wood to feed the fire, and no powerful allies to defend us.

I have made up my mind: I want to kill myself. That is what women in my situation do. I will swallow acid and die, to put out forever the fire of shame that torments my family and me. I beg my mother to help me die. She must go buy some acid so that my life may finally end, since I'm already dead in the eyes of others! My mother bursts into tears, and by staying at my side day and night, she foils my suicide attempt. I can't sleep, and she won't let me die. For several days, I go insane with helplessness. I cannot go on living like this, lying down, shrouded in my shawl! Finally, out of nowhere, a surprising fit of anger saves me from that stupor.

Now it's my turn to seek revenge. I could hire men to kill my attackers. The gang would charge into their home, armed with guns, and justice would be done. But I have no money! I could buy a gun myself, or some acid that I could throw into their eyes to blind them. I could . . . but I am only a woman, and we have no money. We haven't the right to have any! Men have the monopoly on vengeance, which passes through violence inflicted upon women.

Now I learn certain things I hadn't heard about before: the Mastois, who are capable of attacking and robbing anyone's home with their guns, have already committed numerous rapes and have pillaged the house of one of my uncles. The police know all this, and they also know that no one can stand up to the

Mastois, because anyone who dared defy them would be swiftly killed. The Mastois have been here for generations, and there is nothing to be done about them. They have friends in high places, and absolute power is in their hands, from our village all the way up to the district capital. They are in control. Which explains why they could tell the police, when the trouble began, "If you have to release Shakur, you must turn him back over to us!"

Even the police were afraid for my brother's life, and the sole solution they found was to put him in a cell until they could determine his guilt or innocence.

That request for forgiveness I was asked to make in public was therefore doomed from the start. The Mastois agreed to it only so that they could rape me in front of the entire village. They aren't afraid of the mullah, or the devil, or God. Within the tribal system, their superior caste gives them complete freedom to decide who is their enemy—who must be crushed, humiliated, robbed, raped. They attack the weak, and we are the weak.

•   •   •

So I ask God to help me choose between suicide and revenge by any means possible. I recite the Koran. I talk to God the way I did when I was a child. Whenever I'd done something naughty, my mother always said, "Watch out, Mukhtaran! God sees everything you do!"

Then I would look at the sky and wonder if there was a window up there through which God watched me, but out of respect for my mother, I never asked her that question. Children do not address their parents. Sometimes, when I needed to talk to an adult, it was my paternal grandmother whom I would ask to explain *how* and *why* things happened. She was the only person who listened to me.

"Nanny, Mama always says that God is watching me. Is there really a window in the sky that he opens to look at me?"

"God doesn't need to open a window, Mukhtaran. The whole sky is his window! He sees you, and he sees all the others on this earth. He judges your foolishness along with everyone else's. What mischief have you been up to?"

"My sisters and I, we sneaked the stick away from the neighbors' grandfather, and we put it across the doorway to his room. When the grandfather went inside, we lifted up the stick, each on our side, and he fell down!"

"Why did you do that?"

"Because he's always scolding us. He doesn't want us to climb trees so we can swing on the branches, he doesn't want us to talk, to laugh, to play—he doesn't want anything! And he's always shaking his stick at us, as soon as he shows up! 'You, you didn't wash your bum, go clean yourself! You, you're not wearing your scarf! Go get dressed!' He never stops grumbling at us—that's all he ever does!"

"That grandfather is very old, and he's a mean one. He can't stand children, true, but don't ever do that again! What else did you do?"

"I wanted to come eat with you, but Mama wouldn't let me. She says I have to eat at home."

"I'll speak to your mother so that she doesn't bother my granddaughter anymore. . . ."

No one in the family ever beat us. My father never lifted a hand to me. My childhood was a simple one of poverty, neither wonderful nor miserable, but full of joy. I would have liked that period to last my whole life long. I pictured God as a king: he was tall, and strong, seated on a divan, surrounded by angels, and he forgave people. He granted mercy to those who had done good deeds, and he sent the others to hell for their wickedness.

At twenty-eight years old (or close enough, if I believe my mother), imprisoned by shame in this room, God is my only comfort in my loneliness. Death? Or revenge? How can I recover my honor?

While I pray, all alone, rumors continue to course through the village.

People say that our mullah delivered a sermon during Friday prayers. He said right out loud that what had happened in the village was a sin, a disgrace for the entire community, and that the villagers ought to speak to the police.

People say that there was a reporter from the local press in the congregation, and that he recounted the story in his newspaper.

People also say that the Mastois went to a restaurant in the city, where they boasted publicly about their exploits in great detail, thus spreading the news throughout the region.

On the fourth or fifth day of my reclusion, during which I have tirelessly recited the Koran without eating or sleeping, teardrops begin spilling from my eyes for the first time. Finally, I cry. My mind and body, parched and exhausted, find release in slow streams of tears.

As a child, I was carefree, merry, and given to harmless little pranks and crazy laughter, but I have never found it easy to express deep emotion. I can remember crying only once, when I was about ten. An escaped chick, pursued by my brothers and sisters, dashed frantically by mistake into the fire over which I was cooking chapaties, unleavened wheaten bread. I threw water onto the flames, but too late—the chick burned to death before my eyes. Convinced that it was my fault, that I'd been clumsy in my efforts to save it, I wept all day long over the horrible death of that innocent baby bird. I have never forgotten that feeling of guilt, nor has it forgotten me, and even today I feel guilty. Perhaps if I'd been quicker, I might have saved the tiny bird, which would have grown up to enjoy its little life. I felt as if I had sinned by killing a living creature, and now, secluded in my room, I am weeping for myself the way I wept over that dead chick, roasted to death in seconds by the fire.

I feel guilty for having been raped, and that is a cruel feeling, because what happened a few days ago was not my fault. As a child, I did not want that chick to die, just as I did nothing to deserve my shameful punishment. The rapists? They don't feel guilty at all! But I, I cannot forget, and I cannot speak to anyone about what happened to me—it's just not done. Besides, talking about the rape would be unbearable for me, and whenever fresh memories of that appalling night invade my thoughts, I drive them frantically from my mind. I don't want to remember! But I can't help it. . . .

Suddenly, I hear shouting in the house. The police have arrived!

Leaving the room, I see Shakur racing through the courtyard in such a panic that without realizing it, he heads straight for the Mastoi farmhouse! My father runs after him, just as frightened as my brother. I'm the one who must calm them down and persuade them to return to our house.

"Papa, come back! Don't be afraid! Shakur! Come home!"

When my father hears the voice of his daughter—whom he has not seen for several days—just as he catches up with Shakur, he stops, and the two of them return prudently to our courtyard, where the police are waiting.

Strangely enough, I am no longer afraid of anything, and the police don't scare me at all.

"Which one is Mukhtaran Bibi?"

"I am."

"Come here! You must accompany us to the police station right away. Shakur and your father have to come too. Where is your uncle?"

We leave in the officers' car, pick up my uncle along the way, and drive to Jatoi, where we must wait at the police headquarters until the police chief arrives. There are chairs, but no one tells us that we may sit down. The chief, it seems, is asleep.

"You will be called!"

Reporters are there. They ask me questions, wanting to know about everything that happened to me, and suddenly, I'm talking. I tell them my story, without going into intimate details that are no one's business but my own. I tell them the rapists' names, describe the circumstances, explain how it all began with the false accusation against my brother. Ignorant though I may be of the law and our judicial system, which is never accessible to women, I sense instinctively that I must take advantage of the presence of these journalists.

And then someone from our family arrives at the police station in a lather of anxiety: the Mastois have heard that I am at the station, and they are threatening to punish us.

"Don't say anything! You must drop this whole thing. If you do, the Mastois will leave us alone, but if you continue . . ."

I have decided to fight. I still don't know why the police came to get us. Only later will I learn that our story has spread quickly through the nation's newspapers, thanks to that first local article. People have heard of us in the capital, Islamabad, and even elsewhere in the world! Worried about this unusual publicity, the provincial government of Punjab province has asked the local police to prepare a report on the subject as quickly as possible. A full jirga, rejecting the advice of the local mullah, has condemned a woman to be gang-raped. There is public outcry. This makes the Mastois even angrier.

Like many illiterate women, I knew nothing about the law—and so little about my rights that I didn't even know I had any! Now, though, I'm beginning to understand that my revenge can take another path besides suicide. What do I care about threats or danger? What could be worse than what I just went through? My father, to my surprise, supports my decision to fight back.

If I were educated, if I could read and write, everything would be so much easier! I set out anyway, with my family behind me, in an entirely new direction.

The long road ahead of us is completely unfamiliar because in our province, the police are directly controlled by the upper castes. Policemen act as the fierce guardians of tradition, allied with the tribal authorities. Whatever decision a jirga makes will be accepted and backed up by the police. It's impossible to charge an influential family with a crime if the police consider the matter a village affair, especially if the victim is a woman. Most of the time, the police cooperate with the guilty person, whom they do not consider a criminal. A woman is nothing more than an object of exchange, from birth to marriage. According to custom, she has no rights. That is how I was raised, and no one ever told me that Pakistan had a constitution, laws, and rights written down in a book. I have never seen a lawyer or a judge. I know absolutely nothing about the official justice reserved for wealthy and educated people.

So I have no idea where my decision to file a complaint will lead me. For the moment, it's a springboard for my survival, a weapon for my revolt as I seek to avenge my humiliation, a weapon still untested, yet precious to me—because it's the only one I have. I will have justice, or death. Perhaps both.

When a policeman finally sends for me and begins writing down my answers to his questions, I feel another emotion surge through me: suspicion. Three times he goes to consult his superior, whom I never see. Each time, he returns to write a few lines, although I had spoken for a long while. When he has finished, he has me ink my fingertip and press it at the bottom of the page as a signature. It is not my statement, but people will claim that it is.

Even without knowing how to read, or having heard what he asked his boss, I understand that on this mere half a page, he has written what was dictated to him by his superior. In other words, by the Mastoi clan chief. I may not know this for a fact, but I know it instinctively. The policeman does not even read over for me what he has written. It's now two o'clock in the morning, and I do not know whether I have just placed my fingerprint on a document saying simply that nothing happened, or that I lied. I later realize that he had also put a false date on the report.

Leaving the police station in Jatoi, we must make our own way home, some miles away. We find someone with a motorcycle, which is a common form of transportation here, and ordinarily he would have agreed to take us home, but he refuses to take Shakur and me because he is afraid of encountering some Mastois along the way.

"I'm willing to take your father, but no one else."

So the cousin who came from the village to warn us

of the Mastois' threats against us is obliged to accompany us home, but he makes a detour to avoid taking the usual route.

Nothing will be "as usual" from now on. I myself am already different. I don't know how I am going to fight, but I want justice, and that will be my revenge. The direction of my new path, the only one possible, is clear in my mind. My honor, and that of my family, depend on it. Though it might cost me my life, I will not die humiliated. I have suffered for days, contemplated suicide, cried my heart out. I am changing, behaving differently, which I would never have thought possible.

When I begin this journey into the legal system, a path from which there is no turning back, I'm hampered by my illiteracy and my status as a woman. Aside from my family, I have only one strength to call upon: my outrage.

Before, I had lived in absolute submission; now, my rebellion will be equally relentless.

A Most Remarkable Judge

It's five o'clock in the morning by the time we finally get home, and I'm staggering with exhaustion. At such moments, a woman of my modest station in life wonders if she's right to try upsetting the established order of tribal tradition. I now know that the decision to rape me was made in the presence of the whole community. My father and uncle heard that verdict along with all the other villagers, but my family had hoped that in the end, we would be forgiven. In reality, we were all caught in the same trap, and I was already doomed.

Whatever doubts and fears I may feel, it's too late to back out now. Whether they're Mastoi, Gujar, or Baluch, the men of the Punjab have no idea how unspeakably painful it is for a woman to have to talk about such an assault, even though I hadn't gone into detail in my statement to the policeman. The simple word *rape* is enough. There were four of them. I saw their faces. They threw me out of the stable, I tried to cover my half-naked body while the other men watched, and I walked away. The rest is a nightmare I keep trying to forget.

Telling my story over and over—I simply couldn't do that. Because to tell it is to relive it. If only I felt that I could trust someone. . . . With a policewoman, it would be less agonizing, but the terrible thing is, here there are almost no women in the police and the judicial system. Just men.

And our troubles aren't over yet: hardly have we returned home than the police show up again. This time, they take me to the county police headquarters for "formalities."

Since the incident has already been reported in the press, it occurs to me that the authorities may fear the arrival of other journalists, who would spread the news even more widely. I'm not really sure of anything though. Every movement is an effort for me, and feeling other people's eyes on me is sheer humiliation. How can anyone eat, drink, sleep, after such a grueling experience? And yet, I get up, walk outside, and climb into that police car, where I hide my face in my shawl, without even watching the road go by. I have become a different woman.

I find myself sitting on the floor, in the company of strangers, in a room without any furniture. I don't know what I'm doing here or what will happen next. No one comes to take me anywhere to interrogate me.

And since no one talks to me or explains anything at all to me, I have plenty of time to think about the way women are treated. Men are the ones who "know"; women must simply keep quiet and wait. Why tell us anything? Men make the decisions, rule, act, judge. I think of the goats tied up in courtyards to keep them from wandering around the countryside. I don't count for more than a goat here, even if I haven't got a cord looped around my neck.

Time passes. When Shakur and my father arrive to see what's going on, the police shut them up in the same room with me, where we stay all day long without daring to speak. At sunset, the police drive us back to the village. No interrogation; no "formalities." As usual, I have the feeling that I've been shunted aside from something, but I don't know what. When I was a child, and then a young woman, all I could do was listen intently to the grown-ups to try to understand what they were talking about. I could neither ask questions nor speak up on my own—I could only wait to figure out what was happening around me, by piecing together other people's words.

At five o'clock the next morning, the police return and take me to the same room in the same place, where I spend the entire day, only to be driven home again at sunset. On the third day, I spend the same long day in the same room doing nothing. I'm not certain that this imprisonment is due to the presence of journalists in the area, but this suspicion will eventually be confirmed. If I had only known, I would have refused to leave the house. On that third and last day, during the evening, my father, Shakur, and the mullah are brought to the same police station. I don't see them, because we are in separate rooms. Later I will learn that one is for civil infractions, the other for criminal offenses: I was kept in the civil section, the mullah and my family in the other. They will tell me afterward that before my interrogation, all three of them were questioned about what happened. When I'm finally taken away to be interrogated, I encounter the mullah, who has just time enough to warn me.

"Watch out! They write down everything you tell them in their own words."

It's my turn, and as soon as I enter the office of the county police chief, I understand what's going on.

"Look here, Mukhtar, we know the Mastois very well, they are not bad men, but you're making accusations against them! Why are you doing that? There's no point."

"But they grabbed me by the arms, and I shouted for help, I begged for mercy. . . ."

"Silly girl, you must never claim that. Everything you have said up until now, I will write down, and I will read you the preliminary report. But tomorrow, I will be taking you to court, and in front of the judge, you will be careful, very careful: you will say exactly what I am telling you now. I have prepared everything, and I know that it is in your best interest, and in the

best interest of your family, and of everyone concerned."

"They raped me!"

"You must not say that you have been raped!"

There is a piece of paper on his desk, on which he
has already written something. How can I know what
is written there? If only I knew how to read! He has
seen me looking at the paper, and he couldn't care less.

"You must not mention Abdul Khaliq's name. You
must not say that you have been raped. You must not
say that he was the one who did anything."

"But he was there!"

"All right: you may in fact say that Abdul Khaliq
was there. Everyone knows that. You will say, for example, that Abdul Khaliq called out, 'There she is!
Forgive her!' "

That does it. I storm out of the room in a rage.

"I already know everything I must say, because I've
already said it! I don't have to listen to your nonsense!"

And suddenly I'm in the hall, ready to get out of
that place. Humiliated and utterly disgusted. It's clear
to me: this policeman wants me to let the Mastois get
away with rape. He thought he could frighten me into

dropping all charges. Oh, they know them very well, do they? And they are not "bad men"? Half the village knows how bad they can be. My uncle knows it, and my father too. Shakur and I are their victims, and when they are not being bad men they simply prevent people of my caste from buying a few scraps of land so that they can take them themselves. That's what feudal power is. It begins with land, and ends with rape.

I may be poor and illiterate, and perhaps I've never stuck my nose into men's business, but I have ears to hear and eyes to see. Plus a voice to speak—and to speak up for myself!

A police officer has come up behind me. He draws me aside from my father and the mullah, who are still waiting in front of the door to the other office.

"Come over here, listen to me. . . . Calm down, Mukhtaran Bibi. Listen! You have to say what we tell you to say, because it's better for you, and for us too."

I have no chance to reply. Another officer herds my father, Shakur, and the mullah into the office.

"Okay—we have to take care of this right away! You'll sign these, and we'll fill in the report."

He picks up three blank sheets of paper, and shuts

the door behind the three men. Almost immediately, he leaves the room again and comes toward me.

"Your father, brother, and the mullah have agreed, they've signed, and we'll take care of the rest. The fourth page is for you, so you do as they did: just sign with a fingerprint. And we'll write exactly what you said on the paper, no problem. Put your thumbprint here!"

The mullah has signed, and I trust him. So I do as the policeman asks, placing my thumbprint at the bottom of the blank sheet of paper.

"That's fine. You see, it's only a formality. Soon you'll be taken to the courtroom, before the judge. Wait here."

At around seven o'clock, after sunset, two police cars take us away. The mullah goes off in the first one, the other three of us in the second car. Along the way, the policemen receive a message from the judge, who informs them that he can't come to the courtroom because he has guests at his home. He asks that we be brought to his house. Once we get there, he changes his mind.

"No, this won't work, there are too many people

here. It would be better to do this in the courtroom after all. Take them there, and I'll follow you."

We wait outside, in front of the courthouse, and when the judge arrives, I see that a police car has also brought along Faiz and four other people, whom I can't see distinctly in the darkness. Faiz is the only one I am able to make out.

I didn't know that they'd been summoned as well. My family and I don't speak to one another, because of the policemen. Shakur seems sad, utterly defeated. The marks on his face still show what he went through, even though his wounds have stopped bleeding. So far, my brother has told no one except my father what happened to him. I hope that he too will be able to defend himself, but he's young, so young to confront both the police and a tribunal, all on the same day. I wonder if he has been advised, as I was, not to accuse anyone.

Luckily, my father is here. He protects us the way he always has, unlike certain fathers, who would not hesitate to sacrifice their son or daughter to protect themselves from trouble. After he realized that the man chosen to be my husband was a disreputable lout who didn't keep his promises, my father supported me in my divorce. He never wavered, and neither did I, until I had obtained the *talaq*, which can be given only by the husband. It is his agreement to release his wife, and without it, a woman cannot be divorced: her cause must be pleaded before a judge, which is expensive, and not always allowed, in any case. I regained my freedom thanks to my father and to my own stubbornness, the only weapon we women have against men.

My father had truly believed that—according to a tribal law he told me he was sure was written down somewhere—Faiz was supposed to show mercy in a village council. Forgiveness is possible, even when there has been a murder during a family feud. In reality, however, that law favors the powerful: they may forgive an offense, but they are not required to do so. And since the Mastois outnumber everyone else, they run the jirga.

The Mastois did not forgive and forget, and neither will I. The offense they claim to have suffered is nothing compared to what my brother and I endured. The Mastois have no monopoly on honor.

• • •

I stand before the judge: this time I am the first to be interviewed. He is a distinguished man, very polite, and the first official to call for an extra chair so that I may sit down! Instead of lording it over me from his judge's seat, he sits down opposite me, on the other side of a table. He also asks for a pitcher of water and some glasses. We both refresh ourselves, and I'm grateful to him, because it's been a rough day.

"Remember, Mukhtaran Bibi, you are before a judge. Tell me the precise truth, everything that happened. Don't be afraid. I must know what was done to you. You are alone here with me and my assistant, who will write down what you tell me. This is a court of law, and I am here to learn what happened. You may speak freely."

I begin my story, as calmly as I can, but my heart is in my throat. Talking about the rape is excruciating, and the judge encourages me.

"Be careful," he keeps reminding me. "Tell me the truth. Don't rush, don't panic. Tell me everything."

I trust him. I sense from the way this man talks to me that he really is impartial. Unlike the policemen, he hasn't begun by threatening me or by putting words into my mouth. He wants only the truth, and he listens attentively, without contempt. Whenever he sees that I'm becoming upset, shaking, or sweating with emotion, he stops me.

"Take your time, calm down. Have a sip of water."

The interview lasts an hour and a half. The judge wants to know every detail of what happened in that accursed stable. I tell him everything I can, things I haven't yet told my own mother. Then he goes to sit in the seat reserved for the judge.

"You did well to tell me the truth. Now God will decide."

He begins writing, in silence, and I'm so exhausted that I rest my head on the table. I don't want any more questions. I want to sleep. I want to go home.

Then the judge sends for Mullah Razzaq, whom he addresses with the same courtesy he showed me.

"You must tell me the truth. You are a responsible person, I'm counting on you. Don't hide anything from me."

The mullah begins speaking, but his voice quickly

fades away for me: at last I fall suddenly asleep, knocked out by fatigue. I don't remember anymore who came in next, what was said—it's all a blur. I didn't come to until my father awakened me.

"Mukhtar, we're leaving, come on! We have to go."

Just as I was leaving the courtroom, the judge stood up, came over to me, and placed a consoling hand on my head.

"Don't give up. Carry on with courage, all of you!"

The police finally take us back home. I don't see Faiz and the others when we leave, and I don't know whether they were interrogated after us. The next day, however, there are reporters in front of the house, along with strangers, men and women from various human rights organizations. I don't know how they got here or who alerted them. I even meet a gentleman from the BBC, a Pakistani who came all the way from Islamabad! There are so many strangers that I lose track of whom or what they represent. For the next four days, people are constantly coming and going, and our little home has never known such bustle— chickens dashing around the yard, the dog barking, and all of this activity is centered on me.

I speak up without flinching, except if someone asks me for too many details. I have realized that this hubbub in the village can only protect me from the threats of my neighbors, whose farm is within sight of our own. If so many people have come to find out about me, it's because I stand for all the other women in my part of the country who have been violated. For the first time, a woman has become a symbol.

And from these strangers I learn about other rapes, other acts of violence written up in the newspapers. Someone reads me a report, submitted to the Pakistani authorities by various organizations, claiming that in June, more than twenty women have been raped by fifty-three men! Two women have died. One was murdered by her attackers so that she could not denounce them, while the other, in despair because the police had not managed to arrest her assailants, killed herself on July 2, almost the very day on which I myself was questioned by the judge. All this strengthens my determination to keep going, to keep seeking justice and truth, in spite of police pressure and a "tradition" that wants women to suffer in silence while men do as they please.

Suicide is now the last thing on my mind.

"Half the women of our country are the victims of violence," a Pakistani woman activist explains to me. "They're either forced into marriage, or raped, or used as objects of exchange among men. It doesn't matter what the women think, because they're not supposed to think at all! They're not allowed to learn to read and write, to find out how the world around them works. That's why illiterate women cannot defend themselves: they know nothing about their rights, and words are put into their mouths to sabotage their revolt. But we support you! Just have courage. . . ."

That's exactly what the authorities had tried to do with me: "You will say only what I'm telling you to say, because it's in your best interest. . . ."

A journalist mentions to me that the press has discovered a previous complaint against Faiz, filed by a mother whose young daughter he kidnapped earlier in the year, raped repeatedly, and released only when the local press reported my own accusations.

My head is spinning from so much information, and there are all these new faces around me. . . .

• • •

The press is paying so much attention to me only because I'm taking my case to the courts. And in a way, I have also become the public face of a story that actually concerns thousands of Pakistani women.

I'm exhilarated—I feel as though I can finally *see* things all around me as they really are. Beyond my village, beyond the province, all the way to Islamabad, there's a whole world I never knew about. As a child, my longest trips were to neighboring villages where we visited cousins or friends of the family. I remember an uncle who sometimes came to stay with us. He had lived in Karachi since he was a little boy. We used to listen to him, my sisters and I, as he talked about the sea, airplanes, mountains, and the multitudes of people who came from far away. I must have been seven or eight years old, and I had trouble imagining all those strange things. I knew that here, in my village, we were in Pakistan, and our uncle said that to the west, there were other countries, like "Europe." Me, I'd heard only about the English who had occupied our country, but I'd never seen any of them.

And I had no idea that "foreigners" lived in Pakistan. Our village in southern Punjab is so remote, so far from any cities, and I had never seen a television until the day our uncle from Karachi brought one with him. The pictures captivated me: I didn't understand who was behind that weird box that was speaking at the same time I was, even though there was no one else in the room!

The cameras filming me: they're the television. . . . These photographers: they're the newspapers. . . .

In the village, they say that I've been "carried away" by the reporters, who are using me to write articles that are more and more embarrassing for the Punjabi authorities. And that I ought to be ashamed of speaking out, instead of committing suicide or burying myself alive. But all these people who've come here from so many places are teaching me lots of things. For example, that the rape of my brother and then myself was actually a tactic of the Mastois to drive us from the area. The Gujars irritate the Mastois, who don't like it when peasants of our caste buy fields that they think should belong to them. I don't know if this is true, but certain members of my family believe it, because we are in the minority, one that is poorer than the Mastois and without political clout, so it's hard for a Gujar to acquire any land.

And these four days of excitement with the press have made it cruelly clear to me, in the end, how crippled I am by my illiteracy, and by not being able to make up my own mind about important things. That truly hurts me now, even more than my family's relative poverty—I say "relative" because we do at least have enough to eat. To help us survive, we have two oxen, a cow, eight goats, and one field of sugarcane. What infuriates me, though, is that I don't know anything about the written word. The Koran is my one treasure: it is written inside me, in my memory, and it's the only book I have.

Not only that: the children whom I used to teach to recite the Koran, just as I was taught, no longer come to see me. I was once respected as a teacher, but now the village shuns me, wary of too many rumors, too many big-city reporters, too many photographers and newsreel cameras. Too much scandal. For some people, I'm almost a heroine, while for others I'm a leper, a liar who dares to cause trouble for the Mastois. So, in order to fight, it seems that I must lose everything: my reputation, my honor, everything that was once my life. But that's not important.

I want justice.

On the fifth day, the district prefect summons me. Two police representatives arrive to escort me, my father, Shakur, and the mullah to Muzaffargarh. I had hoped that all "formalities" were over for the time being and that justice would do its work, but when I reach the office of the prefect, I find the two county police officers there, the ones who wanted me to say what was "in my own best interest." Is the pressure going to begin all over again? The slightest thing upsets me now, and my face must have betrayed my misgivings. I'd trusted my father and the mullah when I put my thumbprint at the bottom of the policemen's paper, and now I believe that was a trap.

One of the policemen tries to tell the prefect what happened, but the prefect asks both officers to withdraw so that he can speak to me alone.

"My daughter, do you have a problem with these men? Have they wronged you in any way?"

"I have no problem, except that one of them insisted that I place my thumbprint on a blank sheet of paper. He had prepared another one for my brother, my father, and the mullah. And we don't even know what was on those papers."

"Really?"

The prefect is astonished and considers me carefully.

"Do you know the name of the man who did that?"

"No. But I can recognize him."

"Fine. I will have them both return, and you will point him out to me."

He has the two men called back to his office. I'd had no idea that they were also deputy prefects! I point to the man in question, however, after which the prefect dismisses them again without a word.

"I'll take care of him," he tells me. "It seems that they forgot to bring the file they had prepared for me—they're not very well informed about its contents, in any case. I've told them to find it and bring it to me. You will be asked to return here at a later date."

• • •

Three or four days later, the local police arrive to tell us that on the following morning, we'll be taken for another interview.

This time, we are met in Muzaffargarh not by the prefect, but by a doctor from the local hospital. The Mastois, it seems, have now decided to file their own charges, and have brought Salma with them so that she can tell the police that she was raped by my brother, and in fact she arrives almost at the same time as we do, in a separate police car. The doctors will examine both Salma and Shakur. As for me, I still have no idea why I'm here. As a woman, I know perfectly well that it's rather late to be examining Salma. I was looked at by a doctor on June 30, eight days after the fact, and I should certainly have gone to the police earlier, but at the time I was simply incapable of doing so.

To suppress the shame of the crime, the clothing I had worn had already been washed on my mother's orders by the time the police took it away, but I did learn later that the examining physician had confirmed what I already knew, that I had suffered internal injuries, and that he was certain that I had been raped, even though he said nothing about that to me at the time. I was happy to learn that her examination had allowed her to state that I was neither disoriented nor insane! No one, however, can evaluate the private wounds of humiliation, and besides, whether it's because of pride or modesty, I can't bring myself to talk about such painful things.

As for Salma, who claims that she was raped on June 22, it's a bit late for an exam. Unless she was a virgin, which I doubt. So a doctor calls Shakur in for a simple test. He estimates my brother's age at between twelve and thirteen, at the most, which my father already knew.

I'm not present during Salma's exam, naturally, but much later on, thanks to village gossip, I learn that she suddenly changes her tune when the doctor in charge explains to her that he'll be comparing the results of Shakur's exam with those of her own.

"Shakur?" she exclaims. "No, he's not the one who assaulted me! He was holding me by the arms, while his big brother and three cousins raped me!"

The doctor stares at her in astonishment.

"What are you talking about? A twelve-year-old boy would be strong enough to hold you by the arms, all by himself, while three others rape you? Is this some kind of joke?"

The medical team examines her anyway. They estimate her age at around twenty-seven, and note that she has been sexually active for about three years, during which time she has had a miscarriage. In conclusion, the doctors feel that her last sexual relations took place earlier than the presumed rape of June 22.

I don't know exactly how the doctors reach their conclusions, but I learn more about such things every day. What they used for my brother is called a DNA test. And Shakur did not rape Salma. He simply happened to be in the sugarcane field at the same time she was, and the Mastois took advantage of that. The newspapers all say that he was in love with her. Well, it only takes one glance for people to accuse someone of being in love. Girls are supposed to keep their eyes modestly downcast, but Salma—she does whatever she wants. She's not afraid of being looked at, and she even makes sure that she is!

The life I had led until now, teaching the Koran,

was a world away from all these sordid matters. My family raised my sisters and me to respect traditions, and like all little girls, I learned when I was about ten that it was forbidden to speak to boys. I have never broken that taboo. I never got a good look at my husband's face until the day we were married. I would not have chosen him myself, but I respect my family and obeyed their wishes in the matter. Salma, on the other hand, is unmarried and was supposed to be chaste, and her family is up to something: they accuse my little brother first of stealing sugarcane, then of having sex with Salma, and now they're claiming he didn't rape her himself, but that my eldest brother and some cousins assaulted her. I try to be brave, but sometimes I despair over all these lies! How can I obtain justice when these people, my neighbors, endlessly embroider their story, like a shawl that turns a different color every day?

I know what my little brother and I went through.

Shakur told the judge that three men from that family captured and sodomized him, and that he screamed, "I'm going to tell my father, I'll tell the police!" That's when the men threatened to kill him if he talked. Then they dragged him to their farm, locked him in a room, beat him up, raped him again, and handed him over to the police only after the intervention of my father, who had been looking for him for hours.

Here in Pakistan, it is difficult for a woman to prove that she has been raped, since she is legally required to provide four male eyewitnesses to the crime. This is to ensure that the law and chiefly the punishment for rape are not misused. Unfortunately, the only eyewitnesses to both my brother's rape and mine are the criminals themselves!

When the police arrived this morning, I thought they were going to take me to see the prefect on my own, but they drove Shakur and me to the hospital instead. Now I am led into a neighboring office belonging to the president of the general council, where I find a woman waiting for me.

She is a government minister, and she has been instructed to hand me a check for half a million rupees, the equivalent of eight thousand dollars! I'm of a rather suspicious nature, and recent events have obliged me to be even more cautious. I'm afraid the check is a trap.

Listening for a moment to the woman's words of consolation, I stare at the offering in her hand. I take the check without even looking at the numbers: I heard what she said, and it's overwhelming. Half a million rupees! I've never even thought about such a sum. One could buy so many things with this . . . a car, or a tractor, who knows what. . . . Who in my family has ever had half a million rupees? Or even received a check?

Instinctively, without thinking, I crumple the paper and drop it to the floor, not through disrespect for this lady minister, but out of contempt for the check.

"I don't need this!"

You never know: if this lady is giving me so much money, perhaps she has been sent by someone to cover up the affair. But she insists—once, twice, three times—that I take the check. She is well dressed, appears to be a respectable woman, and her eyes don't seem clouded by lies.

"I don't need a check," I tell her in the end. "I need a school!"

She smiles.

"A school?"

"Yes, a school for the girls in my village. We don't have one. If you really want to give me something, then let me say this: I don't need a check, but I do need a girls' school for our village."

"I understand, and we will help you build a school, but at least accept this check to begin with. Share it with your father. I promise you that we will build a school as well. In the meantime, you'll need to pay a lawyer, which will be expensive."

I know this. A Pakistani involved with a women's rights organization told me that a good lawyer can cost twenty-five thousand rupees. And that a trial can last a long time, so the lawyer might ask for even more money. That's why villagers of modest means prefer to appeal to a jirga. The tribal council listens to the plaintiffs, suggests a solution, and the matter is concluded that very day. Ordinarily, no one can lie at the jirga, since everyone knows everyone else in a village, and the head of the jirga delivers a verdict intended to make sure that people in the community do not become lifelong enemies. It was my misfortune that the man who delivered the verdict in my case, against the advice of the mullah, was Faiz. And he divided the village instead of reconciling us all.

So, I accept the check to help pay for my school and legal expenses. Then the woman asks me some questions, very kindly, and I find the courage to inform her, since she is a woman and has an honest face, that my life is in danger. People aren't telling me what my attackers are doing, but I have learned that after being held for a few days at the police station, they've been released. All the Mastoi men are back at home, right up the path from us, waiting for only one thing: to destroy us.

"They're neighbors, their house is just on the other side of a field. I don't dare walk along the path anymore. I feel that they're watching me. . . ."

She doesn't promise me anything, but I can see that she understands the situation. This has all happened quite quickly—even quicker than I can grasp, at the moment. The newspapers have featured my story so prominently over the past four days that the entire country knows about me, including the government in Islamabad. The lady who has just given me the check and promised to help me build a village school is a government official, sent here by the president himself. My picture is everywhere, while my story has appeared in every newspaper here in Pakistan and in many abroad. Amnesty International is aware of me.

On July 4, 2002, a demonstration by human rights groups demands justice. The judiciary criticizes the local police for taking too long to register my complaint and for making me sign a blank report. The police had registered the case on June 30. The judge who interviewed me had said as much to the press, explaining that it was impossible for the police not to have known about the incident even before I'd decided to come forward, and that the jirga's decision was a disgrace. Even Pakistan's minister of justice had stated on British television that the verdict of the jirga, led by the Mastoi tribe, should be considered an act of terrorism, that the tribal assembly itself was an illegal body, and that the guilty should be brought before an antiterrorism court. The affair was, he said, an abuse of power.

The government of Pakistan has therefore decided that the case of Mukhtaran Bibi has become an affair of state. In any case, I am told, the state is supposed to prosecute all criminals irrespective of their influence and status. Eight members of the Mastoi tribe have already been arrested as of July 2, and the police have been ordered to explain their own conduct in the matter. The four guilty parties are on the run, but the authorities are closing in on them. Policemen have been assigned to my home to protect me and my family. In the end, the police arrest fourteen men of the Mastoi tribe. The court has had seventy-two hours in which to decide the fate of the suspects.

It's very strange. The whole world knows my face and is talking about my family's tragedy. Everything is happening too quickly. I can't take it all in. The lady minister told me that my father could take the check she'd given me to a bank in the city of Jatoi, where the director had already been advised that an account should be opened in my father's and my names. I've never had a bank account. And neither has my father. Anxious to safeguard that money, we rush to the bank in Jatoi, where they simply ask us for two signatures and give my father a checkbook.

When we return home in the evening, we find fifteen armed police officers around the house. And the governor arrives with at least fifty people, to encourage me and tell me that the culprits will be punished. He also says that he considers me his daughter, and that I must carry this thing through, that I will be protected.

After a half an hour, he leaves with all his entourage. To me and my father, the governor's words seem empty. He just came for the photos and newspapers. I must fight by myself.

The poor policemen will be forced to sleep out under the trees. Since there are so many people, we'll also have to give them something to eat and drink. As it happens, all those rupees my father and I have cashed will not last long, because the police contingent will remain posted at our house for a year. And only their salaries are paid for by the government.

And since there is always some comic relief in a tragedy, whom do I see arrive, with many members of my family, but a maternal uncle whom I haven't laid eyes on for the longest time—at least since my divorce seven years earlier, in any case. He has a son my age, already married, with children. He had never come before to make an offer of marriage, but seeing me with the governor and my check, he trots one out in the guise of a proverb.

"A broken branch should not be thrown away: it must be kept within the family! If she agrees, I'll take her for my son as his second wife!"

I thank him, without further comment, but the answer is no. What did he want for his son? Me, or the check?

Personally, I want a school.

Breaking the Silence

Pakistani law authorizes the incarceration of any man involved in the crime of rape, whether he took part in it himself or was only a witness. Such men are judged under the regime of Islamic law. The government has set up a special court at the five-county level, however, where the crime can be considered—most unusually—before an antiterrorism tribunal. This works in my favor: I won't have to provide four eyewitnesses to prove that I was raped, which has already been established by medical examination. In addition, a group of village men saw me enter and leave the stable, flung naked into the street in front of everyone.

My safety has been assured; indeed, in a way, I have become the prisoner of my bodyguards, because wherever I go, even for the most trifling reason, I am escorted by the police.

The court has asked to review the entire file. A swift decision would calm public opinion, the national media, and the international press, which has had a field day criticizing the lack of legal rights for women in our democracy because of the reliance here on traditional tribal customs. Human rights organizations, groups opposing violence against women, and NGOs—non-governmental organizations—are all taking advantage of my exemplary case to call attention, through the newspapers, to stories that ordinarily would have escaped public notice. My entire country is on my side. But I only need justice. Simple justice. Nothing more. That will be my revenge. That will be my vindication.

In Lahore, a wife and mother who had asked for a divorce on the grounds that her husband was abusive was murdered in the office of her lawyer, who was himself threatened by the culprit. The murderer is still at large.

Claiming that she had been unfaithful, three brothers burned their sister-in-law alive in a village near Sukkur. The woman was rescued by her father but later died in the hospital.

And the list goes on. Whatever the pretext—divorce, supposed adultery, or a settling of accounts among men—women pay the heaviest price. They may be given as compensation for an offense or raped as a form of reprisal by their husbands' enemies. Sometimes, all it takes is for two men to quarrel about something, and one of them will take revenge on the other's wife. The common practice in our villages is for men to take justice into their own hands, invoking the principle of "an eye for an eye." It is always a question of honor, and they may do as they please: cut off a woman's nose, burn a sister, rape a neighbor's wife.

And even if the assailants are arrested before they manage to kill their victims, the instinct for vengeance doesn't stop there, because other members of their family are always ready to champion the honor of a brother or cousin. I know, for example, that Abdul Khaliq, who is even wilder and more hot-tempered than the others, would never have accepted the idea of letting me go. And no one would have been able to keep him from punishing me—on the contrary: the more extreme the violence, the more driven they are to take part in it.

I don't condone "crimes of honor"; far from it, but

when foreigners hound me with questions, I try to explain to them how society works here in the Punjab, a province where such crimes are unfortunately widespread. I was born in this country, subject to its laws, and I know that I am like all other women who belong to the men of their families: we are objects, and they have the right to do whatever they want with us. Submission is compulsory.

My assailants will be tried by an antiterrorism tribunal, a special court in Dera Ghazi Khan, an administrative center west of the Indus River and more than three hours' drive from the village. The police found weapons in the farmhouse of the Mastois, who probably possess more arms elsewhere, since they had plenty of time before they were caught to hide whatever they wanted wherever they pleased. I don't know if the presence of these weapons is enough in itself to justify this recourse to an antiterrorism tribunal, because many Punjabi men carry weapons. The only advantage for me is that this court is expected to render its verdict swiftly, whereas in an ordinary tribunal, the case could drag on for months or even years.

My presence is required in the courtroom every day, and when I point out that it's difficult for me to go back and forth between Dera Ghazi Khan and Meerwala, lodgings are found for me near the courthouse. I'm not accustomed to the city, to all this dust, these noisy streets with their carts, rickshaws, trucks, and shrieking motorcycles. I will be living here for the next three weeks.

The court begins hearing the case on a Friday in July, only one month after the incident, which is speedy work indeed in our judicial system. The fourteen defendants are brought to the courtroom in handcuffs. Ramzan Pachar is among them. Nine are charged with threatening my father with their weapons; Faiz and the other four are accused of rape. Until now, no man, not even a criminal, has ever been punished for a "crime of honor," so the accused are confident that in the end, they will leave the courtroom as free men. Faiz and the others are silent, leaving their lawyers to speak for them. I find my assailants less cocky than usual, and I'm not afraid to confront them. Yesterday's wolves seem like lambs, but appearances are deceiving. I know what they put me through. They have stopped boasting about their misdeeds and no longer flaunt them as the price of their "family honor."

Before coming here I prayed, as I always do, at sunrise. I believe in God's justice, perhaps more so than in the justice of men. And I'm a fatalist.

Fourteen men of the Mastoi tribe against a single woman of an inferior caste. . . . No one has ever seen such a thing before. Well, the other side has a whole crowd of lawyers, nine in all. I have three, one of whom is quite young, while another is a woman. My chief opponent on the defense team is a skilled speaker who monopolizes the hearings and keeps calling me a liar, saying that I invented everything.

After all, I am a divorced woman, which places me in the lowest rank of respectable females, according to the defense. I even wonder if that isn't why the Mastois chose Mukhtaran Bibi.

The Mastois claim that they offered to exchange women: Salma for Shakur, and Mukhtar for a man of their clan. They insist that my father, my uncle, and Ramzan, the negotiator, refused to go along! On the contrary, however, it appears that Ramzan is the one who suggested that I be delivered to the Mastois for the rape that would equalize the situation between the two families, a proposal my father rejected. This Ramzan seems more and more suspicious to me because of the murky role he played in the affair. In any case, the defense maintains that I have lied from beginning to end. Nothing happened! No one committed *zina-bil-jabar* (under sharia, forcible sexual relations) with the eldest daughter of Ghulam Farid Gujjar, my father.

The defense tries to make me prove that a crime was committed, which I must do. According to Islamic law, there are two ways to obtain this proof: either through the complete confession of the guilty party or parties before a competent court (which never happens), or the testimony of four adult Muslim men known for their piety and considered honorable by the court. But the absence of these prerequisites does not bar a Pakistani court from relying on other corroborative evidence, primarily the medical evidence.

My presence in this exceptional tribunal can only mean, however, that fate has chosen to show me the way to justice. And if the verdict is fair, it will be my revenge. Standing before these cringing men in chains, I'm no longer afraid to testify, coldly, and without extraneous details. The account I gave to the examining magistrate has already been entered as evidence.

It is some time now since I recorded my statement, but I recall having told the trial judge in some detail about my appearance before the jirga. I had heard a man's voice saying, "She must be forgiven," but another man came forward immediately and insisted upon the rape. Only my father, uncle Hadji Altaf, and Ghulamnabi seemed willing to defend me, but they were outnumbered and held hostage by the well-armed Mastois. There were four assailants, who raped me one after the other and threw me out of the stable in a shameful state before the eyes of my father.

When I finish speaking, I appear calm, but my heart and stomach are aching with shame.

The hearings are held behind closed doors. The reporters are waiting outside. Only the accused, the witnesses, the lawyers, and myself—the plaintiff—are present before the judge, who intervenes from time to time when the proceedings become bogged down in arguments among the lawyers.

• • •

At the final hearing, the presiding judge is prepared to render his verdict the following day. As it happens, I am not present when he questions the prefect, as well as the deputy prefect (the one who had me sign my "statement" on a blank sheet of paper) and his men. I later learn that according to the latter, my account at the time differs from my present testimony.

"I summoned you," explains the judge, "because you were all there when Mukhtar told her story, and you are all responsible for what is written on these documents."

"Your Honor," replies the prefect, "allow me to make clear that it was the others who concocted that business. Mukhtar told me about it when she spoke to me in my office earlier in the case, and when I sent for the policeman, he said, 'There's no problem, the paper must be in the dossier, I'll look into it,' but he never brought me that dossier!"

"Hearing that," exclaims the judge angrily, "makes me want to send you off to prison!"

The judge lets him go, however, and announces that there will be a delay in the resolution of the case.

• • •

On August 31, 2002, the court delivers its verdict during a special session outside of court hours. Six men are condemned to death and ordered to pay fifty thousand rupees in damages and costs: four of the defendants for the rape of Mukhtaran Bibi, the other two for the instigation of the rape as members of the jirga, namely Faiz, the clan leader, and Ramzan. This last pretended to be negotiating on behalf of my family, whereas he was actually a hypocritical traitor, taking advantage of my poor father's trust in him, doing everything he could to give the Mastois what they wanted.

The other eight men are set free.

I announce to the journalists waiting outside the courthouse that I am calm and satisfied with the verdict, but that my lawyers will appeal the decision to release the eight Mastoi men. I also hope that the state prosecutor will file a separate appeal. The six convicted men, for their part, will appeal their death sentences. So even though I have won, it isn't over yet. My activists for women's rights are overjoyed anyway—the triumphant struggle of Mukhtaran Bibi is an important symbol for them.

I can return to my village with my head high, and modestly covered with the traditional shawl.

I still have a school to build, and it isn't easy. I don't know why, but sometimes my strength abandons me. I'm losing weight, and my face grows haggard with fatigue. Both the ordeal that destroyed my peaceful life and this resounding victory hailed by the media depress me no end—I'm tired of talking, of having to deal with men and their laws. People say that I'm heroic, when I'm utterly exhausted. I used to laugh and be merry, but I've lost that gaiety. Once I loved to joke with my sisters, and I enjoyed my work, my embroidery, teaching the Koran to children; now I'm sad and listless. With this cordon of policemen in front of my door, in a way I've become the prisoner of my own story, even though I won out over my tormentors.

The lawyers and activists reassure me: the appeal will take a long time, a year or even two, and in the meantime, I'm safe. Even the men who were released don't dare so much as frown at me. And that's true. Thanks to my courage, people say, I've turned the spotlight on the condition of women in my country, and other women will follow my lead. How many, I wonder?

How many will be supported by their families as I was supported by mine? How many will be lucky enough to have a journalist report the facts, to have human rights organizations take up their causes so strongly that the government itself must intervene? There are so very many illiterate women in the villages of the Indus River Valley, so many women whose husbands and families will reject them, leaving them defenseless, stripped of honor and all means of support. It's just that simple.

My ambition to establish a girls' school in the village is very dear to my heart, and the idea occurred to me almost like a gift from God. I was trying to find a way to educate girls, to give them the courage to learn. The mothers in the villages don't do anything to help them, because they can't. Since a girl must help with the housework, the father doesn't plan on sending her to study. That's how things are. And in my remote province, what does a girl learn from her mother? How to make chapaties, cook rice and lentils, wash clothing and hang it up to dry on palm trunks, cut grass for the animals, harvest wheat and sugarcane, prepare tea, put the youngest children to bed, fetch water from the pump. Our mothers have done all these things before us, and their mothers did the same before them. And then it's time to be married, to have children. . . . That's how life goes on from woman to woman.

In the cities, however, and even in other provinces, women can study and become lawyers, teachers, doctors, journalists. I've met some of them, and they don't seem scandalous to me! They respect their parents and husbands, but they have the right to speak for themselves, because they have knowledge. To me, the answer is simple: knowledge must be given to girls, and as soon as possible, before their mothers bring them up the same way they were raised themselves.

I'll never forget the words of that policeman who interrupted when I was ready to give my testimony to the district prefect: "Let me explain it to you! She doesn't know how to say things. . . ."

But I spoke up. Because I have a strong character? Because I was humiliated? Because my tongue was suddenly free to speak? For all of those reasons. But I'll make sure girls learn to read, and I'll learn to read too.

Never again will I sign a blank sheet of paper with my thumbprint.

I had once thought about building a small hospital in memory of a sister of mine, who died suffering from cancer because she received no real medical care. Such an undertaking would cost more than a school, though: hiring a doctor, a nurse, obtaining medicine to be dispensed for free—an impossible headache. When I found myself with the lady minister, I said "school" instinctively, although the idea had never crossed my mind before the incident with the thumbprint. Because in that situation, I felt handcuffed, helpless in the face of events. If I had known what the policeman was writing down, things would have happened differently. He would have tried to manipulate me in another way, but not so openly.

In certain regions, the local policemen and the important officials are pawns in the tribal system, controlled by the wealthy landowners, because in the end, the rich are the ones who rule. I can consider myself a survivor of that system, thanks to my family, the media, a clear-thinking judge, and the intervention of the government. My only brave action was to speak up, even though I'd been taught to be silent.

A woman here has nothing solid to stand on. When she lives with her parents, she does what they want. Once she has joined her husband's household, she follows his orders. When her children are grown, her sons take over, and she belongs to them in the same way. My distinction is to have broken free of that submission. Freed from my husband, childless, I can now seek the honor of taking care of other people's children.

With the help of the government, my first school opens its doors by the end of 2002. The state has been generous, widening the road, improving drainage, bringing in electricity, and I have had a telephone line installed. I spend what remains of the five hundred thousand rupees buying two lots of almost four acres each near my house. I even sell my jewelry for the girls' school, which starts out with the pupils sitting on the ground in whatever leafy shade we can find.

And that's my "school beneath the trees," until we can construct a suitable building. The little girls begin calling me Mukhtar Mai, "respected big sister." Every morning I see them arrive with their notebooks and pencils, and the teacher calls the roll. That success, although still incomplete, fills me with such happiness! Who would ever have said that Mukhtaran Bibi, the illiterate daughter of peasant farmers, would one day be the principal of a school?

The government pays the salary for a teacher in the boys' section, and other contributions arrive later, from Finland, for example: fifteen thousand rupees to provide a teacher's salary for three years.

The end of 2002 finds me with my honor trampled but with an award certificate framed on my desk at the school.

International Human Rights Day
First National Observance of Women's Rights
In Recognition of Mrs. Mukhtaran Bibi
December 10, 2002
The International Committee for Human Rights

I really exist in the world, and in the name of all Pakistani women.

In 2005, after a little more than two years, the school is in full swing. The teachers' salaries have been paid for a year, and I'm planning to construct a stable, so that I can buy cows and goats to provide the school with some independent revenue.

Although my responsibilities weigh heavily on me at times, I receive some welcome moral support when a feminist organization, Women's Club 25, invites me to Spain to participate in the International Women's Conference, chaired by Queen Rania of Jordan. I fly in a plane for the first time in my life, accompanied by my elder brother. Both of us are nervous, especially since the people all around us are speaking so many foreign languages. Luckily, we are warmly welcomed at our stop in Dubai and escorted through the rest of our trip.

Many women attend that conference on violence against women, and they come from so many coun-tries, with so much to say, that I'm stunned by the mag-nitude of the problem. For every woman who resists violence and survives, how many are buried beneath the sand, without dignity, without even a grave? My little school seems so small in this flood of misery, like a tiny stone set somewhere in the world in an effort to change the course of human nature by teaching the al-phabet to a handful of little girls, letting this learning do its work from generation to generation. And by teaching a few little boys to respect their companions, sisters, neighbors. Such a small gesture . . .

But here I am in Europe, that territory somewhere to the west of my village, the place my uncle spoke of when I was a child, and these foreigners know my story! I go from one astonishment to another, somewhat timid, not daring to show how proud I am simply to be there, one woman among others in this great wide world.

Back home again, I feel more courageous about my project to enlarge the school. Whenever I hear a student reciting verses from the Koran beneath the palm trees of Meerwala, or chanting the multiplication tables and the English alphabet, I feel that my life has real meaning. Soon there will also be history and geography lessons. My girls, my little sisters, will be learning the same things that boys study.

This existence, however, is outside me.

After that terrible night in June 2002, I did not have anyone in whom I truly could confide. I became mistrustful, incapable of recovering my former life—the serenity, the laughter, the tranquil journey through the days and nights.

It's 2003, a year later. Electricity now brightens the threshold of our house, and the telephone rings—quite often, actually, since I'm constantly getting calls from NGOs and the media. I answer those calls faithfully, because I always need help with my "school beneath the trees," and we still don't have enough funds to put a roof over its head.

One day, I hear a woman's voice on the phone.

"Hello? Good day to you, Mukhtar! I'm Naseem, from the neighboring village of Peerwala. My father is a policeman, and he's stationed in front of your house. I'd like to hear how he's doing."

Peerwala is twelve miles from us. Naseem's father is part of my security detail, and her uncle works on a canal about three miles away. She explains to me that we're distantly related, because we both have aunts in Peerwala who belong to the same family. Naseem has come home after studies in Alipur, the city where I met the judge who seemed so kind and understanding. Now Naseem is enrolled in law school in Multan.

I have never met Naseem, and she knows me only from what she has read in the press. I send for her father, so that he can speak to her, and in the meantime we just chat a bit. Later she calls again, after I have left to go on a pilgrimage to Mecca, the cherished dream of every good Muslim. When she calls a third time, to invite me to come see her, I ask her to visit me instead, because so many people are already coming to see me these days. I have no idea that Naseem will bring me not only friendship, but also precious aid and support. She has read all about me, and my story interests her from a legal standpoint; at the time, in May 2003, my case was still being appealed at the high court. But if her father hadn't been among the police assigned to protect me, we would never have met. Naseem isn't the kind of person who would have imposed herself on me, like some people who've been attracted by my "notoriety."

From the moment we meet, I find Naseem to be an astonishing woman. She's the complete opposite of me: active, vivacious, clearheaded, articulate, not afraid of people—or of saying what she thinks. And I'm quite struck by one of the first things she says.

"You're afraid of everyone and everything. If you keep on that way, you'll never make it. You have to take things into your own hands."

She has quickly realized that only a miracle is holding me up. The truth is, I'm worn out. It has taken a long time for me to understand certain things, such as what people are saying about me, and what will happen as the court considers the Mastois' appeal of their sentences. I still fear the power of that clan and their connections. Although I have police protection . . . nothing is certain yet, since the other eight Mastoi men are still free and can still hurt me. Sometimes, at nightfall, I peer into the darkness. A dog barks, and I jump. I suddenly notice the silhouette of a man—perhaps an enemy, someone who has switched places with one of the policemen, for example. Whenever I leave the house, I'm flanked by armed men. I hurry into a taxi, from which I will emerge only when I am far from Meerwala. Luckily, I don't have to go through the village, since the family farm is located just at the entrance to our community, the first house before the path leading to the mosque. Most of the houses in this village belong to the Mastoi family, however. And the local press regularly speaks ill of me. I'm a "money-grubbing woman." I have a bank account! I'm a divorcée who would do better to return to her husband. My ex-husband himself is spreading lies about me, claiming that I smoke hashish!

Naseem says that I'm becoming paranoid. Thin, anxious, I need to talk with someone I can trust. That's what happens with Naseem. I finally manage to speak freely about the rape, the brutality, the vicious revenge that destroys a woman's body. Naseem knows how to listen to me, for as long as it takes, whenever I need to talk. In developed countries, there are doctors trained to help a woman put herself back together when she has been shattered, trampled like dirt.

"You're like a baby," she tells me. "A baby learning how to walk. It's a new life: you have to start over at zero. I'm not a psychiatrist, but tell me about your life before, your childhood, your marriage, and even what they did to you. You must talk, Mukhtar, and it's by talking that you bring the good and evil out into the open. You free yourself. It's like washing dirty clothing: when it's all clean again, you can wear it with confidence once more."

Naseem is the oldest in her family, and she has now decided to abandon law to work toward a master's degree in journalism, as an independent student. Although our villages are only a little more than twelve miles apart, our two lives are completely different. She has been able to decide about her own future. Naseem is an activist, she speaks up, and she doesn't mince words when she has something to say. She's not afraid of anybody! Even the policewomen posted in front of the house consider her with amazement.

"Do you *always* say what you think?"

"Always!"

She has made me laugh ever since I met her! And made me think about what I've been going through inside myself without ever putting it into words. My lack of education cripples me that way, and my lifelong submission keeps everything locked within me. But Naseem knows what to say.

"Men and women are equals. We have the same duties. I'm well aware that Islam gives men some superiority, but here, men take advantage of that to dominate us completely. A woman must obey her father, her brother, her uncle, her husband, and finally every man in her village, the province, and the entire country!

"I read your story in the newspapers, and lots of people talk about you. But you—do you talk about yourself? You speak about your misfortune with dignity, and then shut up like a box. This tragedy strikes half the women in our country! They are nothing but misery and submission, and never venture to say what they feel or raise their voices. If one of them dares to say no, she risks her life, or at least a beating. I'll give you an example. A woman wants to go see a movie, and her husband won't let her. Why? Because he wants to keep her in ignorance. Then it's easier for him to tell her any old thing, and to forbid her whatever he wants. A man tells his wife, 'You have to obey me, and that's the end of it!' And she never answers back, but me—I answer in her place.

"Where is it written? And what if the husband's a cretin? If he beats her? She should live her whole life being beaten by an idiot? While he goes on thinking he has any brains?

"The wife doesn't know how to read. For her, the world exists only through her husband. How could she rebel? I'm not saying that all the men are the same in Pakistan, but it's too hard to trust them. Too many illiterate women don't know their rights. You've learned about yours, unfortunately, because you wound up all alone, paying for some 'crime' your brother supposedly committed—so you hadn't even done anything yourself! But you had the courage to fight back. Well, you must continue to resist. This time, however, you have to struggle against yourself. You're too silent, too introverted, too distrustful. . . . You're suffering! You have to break out of this prison where you keep yourself locked up. Mukhtar, you can tell me everything."

I manage to open up to Naseem, and I do tell her all about my life. She knows my story, of course, but in the same way that the police, the reporters, and the judges know it: as a news item a little more important than the rest, culled from the national papers.

She hears what I've never told anyone, listening with friendship and compassion.

The moral and physical suffering, the shame, the desire to die, that chaos in my head when I returned alone along the path to my house to collapse onto a bed like a dying animal . . . I'm able to tell Naseem what I couldn't possibly tell my mother or my sisters, because all I have ever learned since I was a tiny child has been: silence.

Later, when I look at photographs of those days, I will sometimes have trouble recognizing myself. I appear emaciated, haunted, as I do in a picture taken when I first met the representative of the Strengthening Participatory Organization, a Pakistani NGO based in Islamabad. He came all the way to the village to see me, and it is thanks to him that Canada became interested in my school project. In that photo, I am shrunken, so withdrawn that I can barely look at myself.

Ever since Naseem has become my sister in the struggle, I have regained my self-confidence. Now that I am eating again, my cheeks are plumper, and there is a peaceful light in my eyes, because I can sleep.

I'd had no idea that speaking about one's pain, about a secret that feels shameful, can set both mind and body free.

Destiny

I grew up without knowing who I was. Invisible. With the same soul as all the other women in the house. Whatever I learned I stole, whenever I could, from the words of others.

A woman might say, for example, "Did you see what that girl did? She disgraced her family! She spoke to that boy! She has no more honor."

Then my mother would turn to me.

"You see, my daughter, what is happening to those people? That could happen to us too. Be careful!"

Even when girls are very small, they aren't allowed to play with boys. A kid found playing marbles with his little girl cousin gets beaten by his mother.

Later, mothers comment in loud voices, so that their daughters can hear. Often the remarks are meant for a daughter-in-law.

"You don't listen to your husband! You're not serving him fast enough!"

That's how the youngest girls, not yet married, learn what they must and must not do. Aside from prayer and the recitation of the Koran, that's the only education we receive. And it teaches us distrust, obedience, submission, fear, abject respect for men. It teaches us to forget ourselves.

I wasn't mistrustful as a child. Or withdrawn. Or silent. I laughed easily. My only confidante was my paternal grandmother, Nanny, who raised me and still lives with us. In our culture, it's normal to entrust a child to another woman besides the mother.

Grandmother is quite old now, and rather blind. She doesn't know her age, no more than my mother and father know theirs. I have an identity card these days, but Grandmother claims that I'm a year older than this paper says! Here in the village, such things aren't important. Your age is your life, the days going by, the weather. . . .

During the harvest, someone in your family might announce, "You're ten years old now!"

No one knows anyone's age closer than to within six months or a year anymore. You might be confused with the preceding child, or the following one. There are no registry offices in the villages. A child is born, lives, grows up, and that's all that counts.

When I was about six, I began helping my mother and my aunt with everything that concerned the household. If my father brought back some grain for the livestock, I cut some too. Sometimes I went to help him cut grass in the fields. My father had a little shop where he sawed wood, and whenever he did outside work, my brother Hazoor Bakhsh was in charge of the harvest.

In time, the family grew: a sister, Naseem; another sister, Jamal, who left us, sadly. Then Rahmat and Fatima. Finally, a second son for my mother: Shakur. The last boy of the family.

I'd heard my mother say now and then that if for the next child, God were to give her a son and then nothing else, she would make her peace with that. It was a way of admitting that she'd had enough children. Tasmia arrived after Shakur, however, the last little girl.

There's a big difference in age between my two brothers, but the girls are closer. When we had time, we used to invent games with rag dolls, I remember, and we took them very seriously. There were girl dolls and boy dolls, which we made ourselves. We played at discussing future marriages between the dolls. I would take a boy doll, for example, and my sister a girl, and the negotiations could begin.

"You want to give your daughter to my son?"

"Yes, all right, but only if you do the same: you give your other son to my other daughter."

"No, I'm not giving my other son. He's already engaged to my uncle's daughter."

We'd invent quarrels around the marriages arranged by the parents, using what we'd heard grown-ups say. There were dolls representing the adults (parents, eldest brothers, even grandmothers) and little children—a whole family. Sometimes we'd have a good twenty dolls in play, made from all the scraps of cloth found in the house. Girls and boys were distinguished by their clothing: boys wore pants and big white shirts; girls had their heads covered by a shawl or scarf, and we made long hair for them from tag ends of braided rags. We made faces for them, with a bit of makeup, tiny nose studs, and earrings. The jewelry was the hardest to find, because we could only create it using material embroidered with little beads or shiny things, from worn-out garments thrown away by the women in the family.

We'd set up this entire little rag-doll family somewhere off in the shade, far from the grown-ups, because if there had been a small but dramatic argument in the house, we loved to act it out with the dolls, and we had to make absolutely sure that no one could overhear us! To protect our treasures from the dust, we set them up on bricks. And the wonderful complicated business of the marriages could begin again.

"You, you want a fiancé for your niece? He hasn't come out of his mother's belly yet!"

"If it's a son, give him to me. If it's a girl, I'll give you my last son."

"But your son will have to live in my house. And he must bring with him a gram of gold. And some earrings!"

I laugh as I haven't laughed in a long, long time as I tell Naseem about the marriage of a cousin that took place when I was about seven or eight years old. That was the first long trip I'd ever taken in those days. I'd set out with my uncle for a village about thirty miles from our home. There was no road, only a path, and the weather was terrible, a constant downpour. As usual, we were traveling by bicycle, three bikes loaded with everyone in the family. Me, I was perched on the frame of my uncle's bike, while someone else sat on the handlebars, and the last passenger rode on the luggage rack. The rain came down relentlessly, but we children were happy to be going to the ceremony, where we would see our cousins and get to play with them.

During our adventure, however, one of my aunts fell off the luggage rack in all her finery. Her lovely glass bracelets shattered, and she was slightly wounded. Everyone panicked, because she was shrieking with pain and weeping over the tiny glass shards in every color of the rainbow. We had to bandage her arms, and then we children looked at one another and just burst out laughing! Everyone ended up laughing along with us—and we howled like crazy people for the rest of the trip, which took forever. Poor Auntie, she was laughing too, wearing her new "bandage bracelets."

Later, I tell Naseem about my marriage as well.

Even though she's an educated woman, Naseem too must respect tradition, and the family picked out a husband for her a long time ago. He's not exactly her ideal, though. So, without wanting to be disrespectful to her parents, she is trying to get out of this proposed marriage. Without arguing, without causing any trouble. Naseem is twenty-seven, studying for her career, and since her fiancé hasn't given any sign of life lately, she's hoping . . . that he'll give up on his own, that he'll get tired or meet someone else. In any case, she says she'll hold out for as long as she can.

For the moment, she hasn't met the man of her dreams, and that's one of the major taboos in our culture. A young woman does not have the right to choose for herself. Some women who have taken that risk have been threatened, humiliated, beaten, and sometimes even killed, although there are new laws that support this right to choose, in theory. Islamic law does not support this right, however, and each caste has its own traditions. Couples who decide for themselves have huge difficulties proving the legality of their marriage. The woman, for example, may be accused of *zina*, a sin that includes adultery and sex without the sanction of marriage. She may then be condemned to be stoned to death. We are constantly being caught between the different legal systems of our religion and our government, not to mention—for extra complications—the tribal system, since each tribe has its own rules that completely ignore the official law, and sometimes even religious law.

As for divorce, that's complicated as well. Only the husband may grant a divorce. When a woman begins proceedings to obtain a divorce in a state court of law, the husband's family may then consider itself "dishonored" and demand "punishment." On top of which, recourse to the official law courts doesn't always lead to a legal decision.

In my case, things turned out differently, and I obtained the divorce I wanted. That's when I found out that I was eighteen years old when I got married.

I remember my sister Jamal coming up to me, giggling.

"Your in-laws are here," she whispered in my ear.

I was torn between feelings of joy and shyness. Joy, because I was going to be married and begin a new life;

shyness, because my sister was laughing, my girl cousins were making jokes, and I was supposed to join in the lighthearted fun over this great announcement, just as if it didn't interest me at all.

"Your Prince Charming is here. . . ."

"Let him go look somewhere else!"

In any case, everything does happen *somewhere else*—among men. All the uncles, brothers, male cousins are gathered together, including the groom's family. Someone suggests a date, and the discussion begins, because they must find a day that is convenient for everyone, that fits in with the moon, plantings, harvests.

"Not Friday," someone may say. "Another cousin is getting married."

"Sunday, then."

"No, not Sunday!" another man protests. "It's my turn to fetch water to irrigate my field, I'm not free."

Finally, they choose a date to everyone's satisfaction. The women have no right to speak up. Still less the fiancée.

That evening, the head of the family comes home to announce the news to his wife, and that's how a girl learns that she will be married on a certain day. I don't remember the day or month of my wedding, but I do know that the date was set for one month before the beginning of Ramadan.

When I learned my future husband's name, I tried to remember him. I'd met him casually somewhere, along a road or during a ceremony. I could recall that he limped heavily, like someone who'd had polio. I didn't say anything to anyone, of course. I just thought, "Oh, so he's the one. . . ."

I was nervous, though. It wasn't my father who had chosen this husband, but my uncle. And I wondered why he was marrying me off to that particular man. Why was he giving his niece to him? I suppose his face was handsome enough, but I didn't know him, and he limped!

When Naseem asked me if I liked him anyway, I was taken aback—I wasn't used to answering such questions. But she laughed and still wanted to know.

"I didn't like him much. If I'd been able to refuse, I would have."

The only thing I knew about him was that his parents were dead. And that he'd come to our house with his elder brother. Once the date was fixed, I was auto-matically engaged. Now advice began pouring ritually from every woman's mouth, and it was always the same.

"You'll be going to your husband's house. Try to bring honor to your parents, to your family's name."

"Do whatever he asks of you. Respect his family."

"You are his honor, and that of his family. Remember that."

Our mothers tell us nothing. We're supposed to know what goes on in a marriage. In fact, I wasn't worried about the idea of deferring to a husband, because all women do in Pakistan. As for the rest, it was a mystery that married women do not share with girls. And we have no right to ask questions. Anyway, getting married and having babies are ordinary facts of life. I've seen women give birth, I know everything I need to know. People speak of love in songs and in other countries, but that's not for me. One day I saw a movie on the television at my uncle's: a beautiful woman wearing lots of makeup and waving her arms around kept stretching out her hands to a man who was making her cry. I speak only Saraiki, a minority dialect, and the movie was in Urdu, our national language, so I had no idea what she was saying. But I thought she was making a huge spectacle of herself.

For us, everything is simple, planned in advance. My parents took care of the dowry, and my mother had been collecting little things for my wedding for several years, such as jewelry, linens, clothing. The furniture is dealt with at the last moment. My father had a bed made for me. On my wedding day, according to strict tradition, I wore a garment that my husband-to-be had bought for me. In our culture, the bride wears red, which is highly symbolic and quite important. Well before the ceremony, the bride must plait her hair into two long braids, and a week before her marriage, the women of the groom's family arrive to unplait them. The women bring along with them all the food the bride will eat during that last week. I don't know what this double ritual means, but I went along with it, and on my wedding day, my hair was beautifully wavy.

In the ritual of *mehndi*, the women of my future family put henna on the palms of my hands and the soles of my feet. Then came the shower, and the dressing of the bride: ample trousers, a long tunic, a large shawl, and all in red. In honor of the occasion, I also wore the burka, which I'd already worn to go out and visit family, so I was used to it. Sometimes I would wear it when I left the house, and when I got far enough away, I would uncover my face, but if I saw anyone in my family, I would replace the burka, out of respect. It's not hard to see while wearing it, because the holes are distinctly larger than the ones in the burkas worn in Afghanistan. It isn't a convenient thing to wear, obviously, but here women wear it only before marriage, and many married women abandon it.

My maternal grandfather, who was polygamous, always used to say, "None of my wives wore the veil. If she wants to wear it, that's her right, but in that case she would have to wear it until the end of her days."

Ordinarily, the mullah arrives to solemnize the union either on the day of the *mehndi*, or on the wedding day itself. In my case, it was the day of the *mehndi*. When the mullah asked me if I accepted the groom as my husband, I was so emotional that I couldn't reply either yes or no! I just couldn't get a word out, so the mullah pressed me for an answer.

"Well? Tell me! Tell me!"

The women there had to make me nod to signal yes.

"She's shy," they explained, "but she said yes, that's it!"

On my wedding day, after a meal of meat and rice (of which I didn't eat a single mouthful), we had to await the arrival of the groom's family to take me away. In the meantime, there were a few more rituals.

My eldest brother had to place a dab of oil on my hair and a bracelet of embroidered cloth on my arm. A woman held a small pot of oil, and my brother had to give her a coin to serve himself first. After him, all my family took turns dipping their fingers in the oil and touching it to my head.

The groom was now allowed to make his entrance into the house. I had not really met him yet, and he would not see my face beneath the burka. I waited, sitting among my sisters and girl cousins, whose job it was to prevent him from entering until he had given them a small bill. Once he had paid them, he was permitted to come through the door. He sat down next to me, and my sisters brought him a glass of milk on a tray. After draining the glass, he slipped them another small bill. Then the ritual of the oil began again, this time with variations. The woman in charge of the oil pot dipped little bits of cotton in the oil and flung them in the groom's face, saying, "Here are flowers for you."

Then she placed another ball of cotton in the palm of my right hand, which I had to clench as hard as I could so that the groom could not open my fingers. It was sort of a test of strength: if he manages to open my hand, too bad for me, he has won. If he can't, everyone laughs at him.

"Some man you are—you can't open her hand!"

He is then obliged to ask me what I want.

"If you would like me to open my hand, you owe me a piece of jewelry."

And the bride can play the game all over again, with the women closing her hand on the cotton ball and the husband trying once more to open her fingers. The sisters, cousins, and all the girls around usually encourage a triumphant bride, shouting, "Ask him for this, and that. . . ."

I closed my hand the first time, and he couldn't open it; the second time, he still had no success, and the women booed him.

I don't know if this ritual has a symbolic value, or if

the husband is supposed to fail, because by custom he must offer at least one item of jewelry. The struggle is real, in any case—you must be strong to win.

There are also songs, which the girls address to the eldest brother. He is the one whom the girls of the family love and respect the most after their father, and it is he who symbolically gives his sister to another man.

I don't remember exactly what the girls sang to my brother—perhaps these words:

> *I look to the south*
> *It seems so far away*
> *Suddenly my brother appears*
> *He's wearing a beautiful watch*
> *He walks with pride in his step.*

This kind of naive song will probably disappear, since girls now listen to the radio, but respect and love for an elder brother will remain unchanged.

The entire family was happy, and so was I, because it was a celebration. But I was also anxious and sad, for I was about to leave the house where I had spent almost nineteen years. It was over: I would no longer be truly *at home* there. The childish games, the playmates, the brothers and sisters—all gone! I was taking a momentous step, and leaving everything behind me. I was worried about the future.

The groom stood up. My girl cousins took me by the arms to lift me up, in the customary gesture. They led me to a large cart, pulled by a tractor. And, still following custom, my eldest brother lifted me in his arms to settle me in the back of the cart.

A small child was waiting in front of the door to the family house of the groom, who must lead the child inside by the hand. Someone gave me the *mandhani*, the tool used to churn butter, and I followed my husband inside. The last tradition, which is called *ghund kholawi*, was that I should not remove the burka until my husband had given something to the little girls who were teasing him.

"Come on, pay up, don't take off the *ghund* until he's given us two hundred rupees."

"No, no, five hundred rupees!"

"No—don't take off the *ghund* unless he gives us a *thousand* rupees."

He went as high as five hundred rupees, which was

a lot at the time, enough to buy a baby goat. And he finally saw my face.

There were four beds in the room where we were to sleep. We would not be alone.

That's how I spent three nights in my brother-in-law's home before going to my husband's one-room house. Then he wanted to go back to his brother's place—he couldn't live without him! Unfortunately, the brother's wife really disliked me and was always trying to make trouble by accusing me of doing nothing, when she was the one who kept me from doing anything!

Since the marriage contract set up by my family had specified that my husband should live with us, I returned home after barely a month of that strange marriage, and my husband did not come with me. He wanted his brother and refused to work with my father. I wonder if he even wanted me at all, because I didn't have much trouble getting the *talaq* from him, the divorce through which he "released me." I gave him back his jewelry. Although a divorced woman, in our culture, is not well looked upon, at least I was free. I had to live with my parents, since it's impossible for a

woman to live alone without acquiring a bad reputation. I worked to help repay my family for the cost of
my upkeep. Between teaching the Koran to the village
children and embroidery to the women, I recovered
my honor and respectability in the community. My life
was peaceful.

Until that evil day on the twenty-second of June.

The tribal justice system at the heart of a jirga is rooted
in ancestral custom, which can be incompatible with
religion and the law. In the case of crimes of honor, the
Pakistani government itself took the step of advising
the provincial governors and police to "obligatorily"
record an "initial report," both to facilitate the investigation and to prevent the guilty from shielding themselves behind the verdict of a jirga in the event of a
serious crime.

And the police constantly sought a signed blank
piece of paper from me! The local police had intended
to compose my complaint at their convenience, thereby
avoiding any conflict with the dominant caste.

This injustice, this base cowardice, was the work of

men. In village councils, the men who assemble to resolve family conflicts are supposed to be sages, not
shameless brutes. When I stood before the jirga, a hot-
headed young man filled with the overweening pride
of his caste, drunk on violence and the desire to cause
harm, was able to have his way. Wiser village elders
were no longer in the majority.

And women have always been excluded from
meetings, even though they are the ones—as mothers,
grandmothers, the custodians of daily life—who understand family problems the best. Men's contempt
for their intelligence is what pushes women aside. I
don't dare hope that one day, even in the distant future, a village council will accept the participation of
women.

What is more serious is that women are the ones
exchanged as merchandise to help resolve conflicts and
exact punishment. And the punishment is always the
same. When sexuality is taboo, when a man's honor in
Pakistani society is centered in women, the only solution he can find to settle all scores is compulsory marriage or rape. This behavior is not what the Koran
teaches us.

If my father or my uncle had agreed to cede me in marriage to a Mastoi, my life would have been close to hell. In the beginning, that sort of solution was intended to reduce confrontations among castes or tribes by intermingling their bloodlines. The present reality is quite different. Married under such conditions, a wife is even more mistreated, rejected by the other women, trapped in slavery. Even worse, certain women are raped to settle financial scores, or simply because of jealousy between two neighbors, and when the victims try to obtain justice, they are accused of adultery, or of having instigated an illicit relationship themselves!

My family is perhaps somewhat different from most, however. I don't know the history of the Gujar caste in the Punjab, or where my tribe came from, or even what its traditions and customs were before the partition between India and Pakistan. The ancestors of our community were both farmers and warriors. As I mentioned earlier, the official language of our nation is Urdu, and many educated Pakistanis speak English, but here we speak only Saraiki, a minority dialect concentrated in southern Punjab.

• • •

Naseem has become my friend—she knows absolutely everything about me. I'm still afraid of men, and I don't trust them, but she's not scared of them.

Aside from the need to educate girls, to give girls the chance to reach the outside world through literacy, the most important thing I've discovered is self-knowledge: the knowledge of oneself as a human being. I have learned to *exist* and to *respect myself* as a woman. Until now, my rebellion was instinctive: I was trying to save myself and my family from danger. Something inside me refused defeat. Otherwise, I would have given in to the temptation of suicide. How does one survive dishonor? How does one overcome despair? With anger, at first, with an instinct for revenge that resists the tempting solution of death, an instinct that allows one to recover, go forward, act. A stalk of wheat beaten down by a storm can spring up again, or rot where it lies. At first I stood back up alone, and gradually I realized that I am a human being with legitimate rights. I believe in God, I love my village, the Punjab, and my country, and I would like to change things for this country, and all the victims of rape, and future generations of girls. I wasn't really an ardent feminist, although the media considered me one. I became one through experience, because I am a survivor, a simple woman in a world ruled by men. But despising men is not the way to win respect.

The solution is to try to fight them as equals.

Mukhtar Mai standing at the entrance of her school; a sign says "Mukhtar Mai School for Girls"

A bed is provided in a classroom for foreign guests

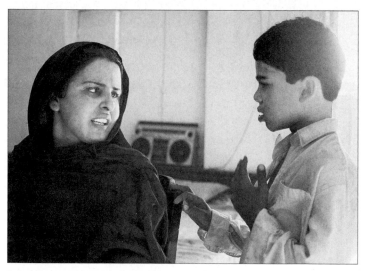

Mukhtar Mai speaks with a student

A classroom full of eager students

Naseem Akhtar (left) and Mukhtar Mai

A chalkboard outside the school illustrating a mathematical equation

Mukhtar Mai seated in one of her classrooms

Students fill the classroom

Originally students used wheat sacks for classroom chairs; now they have wooden desks and chairs

A group of girls study together

Naseem Akhtar (principal at the schools) and Mukhtar Mai

The Way Things Were in Meerwala

No one had ever heard of my village, lost on the plain of the Indus, in the southwest of Punjab, in the district of Muzaffargarh. The police station is in Jatoy, three miles away, and the closest large cities, Dera Ghazi Khan and Multan, are around three hours away by car on a road always jammed with huge trucks, over-loaded motorcycles, and heavy carts. There are no stores in Meerwala, and there was no school.

The arrival of the Mukhtar Mai School arouses the curiosity of the villagers. A suspicious curiosity, at first, and I have only a few pupils. With Naseem's help, I must go from door to door to convince parents to en-trust their daughters to us. These doors aren't slammed in our faces, but the fathers let us understand that girls are made for the house, and not for studies. The boys have more possibilities. Those who don't work in the fields might already be attending school in another village, but no one was forcing them to go.

These diplomatic approaches take a lot of time. And there is no question, naturally, of having a little chat with the Mastoi family. The eldest sons are in prison "because of me." And if the police ever leave me without protection one day, I know the clan would take advantage of that in a second. They keep announcing to anyone who will listen that they intend to take revenge on me and my family.

The construction of the school was of a piece, in the beginning, with our means: simple and straightforward. The furniture came later, and I'm sorry that a few children, including the youngest, are still obliged to sit on the ground. Fortunately, I've managed to buy some large fans that give the children a little relief from the flies and the heat.

I have only one schoolteacher at first: a woman. Thanks to a newspaper article written by Nicholas D. Kristof of *The New York Times* that appeared in

December 2004, the school attracts the attention of Canada's High Commissioner to Pakistan in Islamabad, Mrs. Margaret Huber. Canada has been cooperating with Pakistan on matters of health, education, and good governance since 1947, and changes in the political regime have not interrupted this cooperation, implemented with the help of local Pakistani NGO representatives. Canada has spent millions of dollars in development aid here.

Mustafa Baloch, an official of Strengthening Participatory Organization, comes to Meerwala after a while to see how the school is coming along, and in early 2005 Mrs. Huber also comes all the way to the village, with an entourage of reporters, to personally hand me a check for 2,200,000 rupees, her country's contribution to the construction of the school.

This lady congratulates me for my courage, for fighting to promote equality and women's rights, and for my wish to devote my life not only to justice, but also to education.

I began construction with the funds that I had already received: the five hundred thousand rupees from the Pakistani government, and some private donations sent from the United States. At last, my pupils now study not in the open air, but in a real schoolhouse. A gift from the Canadian International Development Agency (CIDA) paid for the salaries of five teachers for one year, the construction of a principal's office and a small library, plus two classrooms for boys, away from the girls' section. To save money, I bought wood and hired a carpenter to make tables and chairs. Then I began work on a stable, where goats and cows will generate a steady income, independent of donations, because foreign aid doesn't last forever. I already have between forty and forty-five girl students, and classes for both boys and girls are free.

At the end of 2005, I can be proud of the results: a hundred and sixty boys and more than two hundred girls attend the school. All those girls . . . I've won!

But I must still convince their parents to let them come to school on a regular basis. Too often, the villagers make their girls do housework, especially the older ones. So we came up with the idea of creating an attendance prize, to be awarded at the end of the year to the boy or girl who hasn't missed a single day in school: a goat for the girls, a bicycle for the boys.

I now have a small "estate," centered on my parents' former house, where I was born and where I still live. There is a large courtyard behind the women's quarters, and I have added a playground open to the sky, along with four classrooms for girls. The school has five girls' teachers, paid for by outside donations, and one teacher for the boys, funded by the state. Someday, perhaps, the government will also pay the women teachers' salaries. There's always hope. . . .

We have a spacious office, with a small but sufficient library where I keep the important files, the textbooks, and the roll book.

Outside there is a water pump for everyone's use and a men's toilet. In the courtyard, there is another pump for housekeeping use, and a hearth. Naseem is our headmistress, and Mustafa Baloch is our technical advisor regarding organization and construction, because CIDA periodically checks to see how the work is getting on. We're in business! I'm the principal of the only girls' school in my area, set among date palms and fields of wheat and sugarcane. The center of the village is at the end of a dirt path; from my office door I can see the mosque, and from the back of the house, walking through the goats' stable, one can see the Mastois' farmhouse. Their girls and boys come regularly to sit in the school, and I have received no direct threats. The school is peaceful.

The pupils here belong to several tribes, including high and low castes, but at their tender age, the children get along well together. Especially the girls: I have never heard a single mean-spirited remark from any of them. Classes for the boys are held at a distance from my little domain, so that the girls won't encounter them on the path.

And every day, I hear the girls reciting their lessons, running, laughing, chatting on the playground. All those voices comfort me, nourishing my hopes. My life now has some meaning. This school ought to exist, and I will keep fighting for it. In a few years, I hope, these little girls will have enough ideas about education to consider their lives in a new light. Because ever since the dreadful attack that sent the name of my village all around the world, similar horrors against women have not ceased. Every hour in Pakistan, a woman is assaulted, beaten, burned with acid, or killed in the "accidental" explosion of a cooking-gas canister. The Human Rights Commission of Pakistan has recorded

150 cases of rape during the last six months in Punjab alone. And I regularly receive visits from women who come to me for help. Naseem tells them to seek assistance from women's aid associations and gives them legal advice, recommending, for example, that they never sign a deposition without a witness.

Naseem also keeps me up to date on a few stories that appear in the press, because although I can sign my name, compose a little speech, and am learning to read, Naseem reads a lot faster than I do!

"Zafran Bibi, a young woman of twenty-six, was raped by her brother-in-law and made pregnant. She has not repudiated the child and in 2002 was sentenced to be stoned to death, because the child represented proof of *zina*, the sin of adultery. The rapist has gone scot-free. Zafran Bibi is in prison in Kohat, in the northwest of Pakistan, where her husband regularly visits her and demands her release. She will not be stoned but risks spending several years in prison, whereas her rapist is protected by the law."

Here's another one: "A young woman married for love—in other words, she decided on her own to marry the man she loved, against the wishes of both her family and that of her intended fiancé, who therefore considered her 'ill-bred.' During a family reunion, her two brothers murdered her husband, to punish him for having stained the family honor."

No young woman has the right to think about love, to marry the man she would like for her husband. Even in the most enlightened families, women have the duty to respect their parents' choice. And so what if that choice was made when they weren't even born yet! In recent years, jirgas have condemned young women for trying to wed freely, even though our national Islamic law permits this. Bureaucrats prefer to side with tribal laws, however, instead of protecting these women. And the simplest thing for a "dishonored" family to do is to claim that the freely chosen husband has raped their daughter. Faheemuddin, of the Muhajir caste, and Hajira, of the Manzai caste, got married, but Hajira's father had opposed the match, so he filed a complaint of rape. The newlyweds were arrested, but during her husband's trial, Hajira testified that she had not been raped and had married him willingly. The court sent her to a women's shelter while it deliberated her fate. On the very day when the couple won their case at the Supreme Court in Hyderabad, a group of men including the young woman's father, uncle, and brother attacked them as they were leaving the court-house. The couple tried to flee in a rickshaw but were both killed.

Mixed marriages are rare, but Naseem told me about the case of a Christian woman who had married a Muslim and then converted to Islam. She had a daughter with him, who grew into a young woman of seventeen named Maria. One day, an uncle in the fam-ily came to their house claiming that his wife was ill and had been asking for Maria. When the teenager dis-appeared, her mother searched for her in vain. It turned out that the girl had been locked in a room and fed by an old woman for months, without any explana-tion for her imprisonment. Finally, armed men ap-peared with a mullah and forced her to sign a marriage contract and a statement of conversion. Maria was re-named Kalsoom, then taken to the home of her "hus-band," an Islamic extremist who had paid twenty thousand rupees to have her kidnapped. The girl found herself in a new kind of prison, watched by every woman in the house as well as mistreated and in-sulted because she was a Christian.

The poor girl had a child and tried to flee, but was

caught and severely beaten. Finally, when she was pregnant again, she slipped out an unlocked door and after three years' imprisonment, managed to escape and take refuge with her mother. The husband was an influential man, however, who refused to grant a divorce and demanded custody of his child. Maria had to live in hiding, because the lawyer specializing in this kind of divorce, between spouses of different religions, had refused to pursue the case. Before withdrawing, he warned the mother and daughter: the man's family was quite powerful, and the two women were in danger. The husband had paid thugs to kidnap her back. The lawyer was able to do only one thing for her—find her someplace to hide.

This young woman was the child of a mixed marriage, and her story was reported in the press. A report from the Human Rights Commission of Pakistan claims that 226 Pakistani girls, all minors, were kidnapped in Punjab under similar conditions to be forced into marriage. In general, after a first refusal from a girl, the petitioning family undertakes to restore everything "to order." Since a refusal is considered an attack on the family honor, which too often leads to murderous reprisals, both families appeal to a jirga to decide the question. And when there are deaths on both sides, the cost of reconciliation is calculated either in rupees or in the payment of a woman or two. . . . Naseem says that we're less important than goats, or even worse, less important than the slippers a man throws away and replaces when he decides they're worn out.

To resolve a conflict involving murder, for example, one jirga decided to "attribute" two little girls of six and eleven to the victims' family. The older girl was married to a forty-six-year-old man, and the younger one to a victim's brother, a child of eight. And both families accepted the transaction! To resolve a stupid murder that began with a quarrel between neighbors over a barking dog! The members of a jirga usually feel that the best way to calm deadly turmoil in a village is to give a girl or two in marriage, to create bonds among the enemies.

Well, a jirga's decision is nothing but the result of haggling. Such assemblies strive for reconciliation, meeting only to achieve agreement among all parties to a dispute, not to deliver justice. This is the system of "an eye for an eye." If one clan has killed two men, the other has the right to do the same. If a woman has been raped, her father or brother has the right to rape a woman of the other family in revenge.

Most conflicts that don't directly involve men's honor are resolved financially—even murders. This relieves the police and judicial system of a large number of cases. It isn't uncommon—and I'm perhaps the proof of this—to have an earlier quarrel over land annexed by a tribe mysteriously reappear as an honor crime, one the village council can handle more easily, and without requiring the payment of a single rupee.

The big problem for women is that no one informs them about anything. Women do not take part in any deliberations because a village council is formed only of men. Whether a woman is the object of the conflict or the compensation for the offense, she is, on principle, sidelined. She is told from one day to the next that she has been "given" to such-and-such a family. Or, as in my case, that she must beg forgiveness from this or that family. As Naseem says, the dramas and conflicts in a village are true knots untangled by councils without respect for our official laws, especially those regarding human rights.

In January 2005, when I had been awaiting the

judgment of the Court of Appeals in Multan for two years, another incident made headlines in all the newspapers, and commentators compared the story to mine, even though they were quite different.

Dr. Shazia Khalid, a cultured woman of thirty-two, a wife and mother, was working as a physician for Pakistan Petroleum Limited (PPL), a public corporation in Baluchistan. On January 2, her husband was abroad, so she was alone in her house, a walled and guarded property, since the PPL exploitation sector in that area was in a remote tribal zone.

While she was asleep, a man entered her bedroom. She tells what happened next in her own words.

"While he was yanking me around by my hair, I struggled, I shouted, but no one came. When I tried to grab the telephone, he struck me on the head with the receiver and tried to strangle me with the cord. 'For the love of God,' I begged him, 'I've never harmed you— why are you doing this to me?' And he said, 'Be quiet! There's someone outside with a jerrican of kerosene, and if you don't keep quiet, he'll come burn you alive!'

"He raped me, then tied my scarf over my eyes, struck me repeatedly with the butt of his rifle, and raped me again. Then he threw a blanket over me, bound my wrists with the telephone cord, and watched television for a little while—I could hear the sound in English."

Dr. Shazia lost consciousness for a time, then managed to free herself and run to safety at the home of a nurse.

"I was unable to speak—right away, she understood. Some physicians from the PPL arrived. I expected them to take care of my wounds, but they did nothing of the kind, on the contrary. They gave me some tranquilizers, flew me secretly to a psychiatric hospital in Karachi, and advised me not to try contacting my family. I was still able to get through to my brother, and I filed my complaint with the police on January 9. The military information service assured me that the culprit would be arrested within forty-eight hours.

"My husband and I were installed in a different house, which we were forbidden to leave. The president said on television that my life was in danger. The worst of it was, my husband's own grandfather announced that I was a *kari*, a stain on the family. He said that my husband should divorce me, and that I should be expelled from the family. I was afraid of being killed! I tried to commit suicide, but my husband and son prevented me from doing so. Then I was urged to sign a declaration saying that I had received assistance from the authorities and that I had decided to press the matter no further. I was told that if I did not sign, my husband and I would probably be killed. That it would be better if I left the country, without demanding an explanation from PPL, a demand that would then cause serious difficulties for us. I was also strongly advised not to contact any humanitarian or human rights organizations."

The incident had caused quite a stir in Baluchistan, where workers regularly show their hostility to the gas exploitation operations in their region. After a rumor spread that Dr. Shazia's assailant was in the army, a military unit in the sector was attacked. About fifteen men were supposedly killed, and some gas company equipment was damaged.

Today, Dr. Shazia lives in exile somewhere in England, in the midst of a particularly strict Pakistani community where she does not feel at ease. Her husband supports her, but their great sorrow is that they had to leave their son in Pakistan: the authorities would not allow him to follow them. They have lost their way of life and their country, and their only hope, for the moment, is to obtain permission to immigrate to Canada, where they have some family.

Naseem comments on this case with her usual frankness.

"No matter what her social status, whether she's educated or illiterate, poor or well-off, any woman victimized by violence is also the victim of intimidation. With you, it was, 'Put your thumbprint here, we'll write down what's needed!' For her, 'Sign there, or you'll both die!' Whether he's a peasant or a soldier, a man rapes as he pleases whenever he wants. He knows that most of the time he'll be spared, protected by a whole system—political, tribal, religious, or military. We women are not even close to enjoying our legitimate rights. On the contrary! Feminists are not respected: people take us for dangerous revolutionaries at worst, and at best for troublemakers in a man's world. You? They reproach you for turning to feminists—some papers even say that you're being manipulated by reporters and the NGOs. As though you weren't intelligent enough to understand that the only way to obtain justice is to demand it, loud and long!"

I've become a survivor and an activist. An icon. The symbol of the struggle waged by the women of my country.

The Performing Arts Academy of Lahore, it seems, has staged a play inspired by my wretched story—*Mera Kya Kasur (Is It My Fault?)*. The plot isn't based on what happened to me, because the story begins with the daughter of a feudal lord falling in love with an educated young man who is—unfortunately—a farmer's son. They are seen holding hands, so the verdict of the jirga, intended to restore the lord's honor, decrees that the young peasant's sister will be given to the lord's son. The peasant girl kills herself, as does her mother; the young man goes mad and kills himself as well.

Before dying onstage, the young actress who plays "my" role, the woman who is "disposed of," wonders if it really is a sin in her country to be born poor and a girl.

"Will arresting the guilty ones restore my honor?" she exclaims. "How many girls are there like me?

More than suicide—it's the desire for justice that has given me back my honor. Because a person should never feel guilty for someone else's crime."

Unfortunately, not enough women are lucky enough to be able to galvanize the media and human rights organizations.

In October 2004, a large demonstration united hundreds of activists and representatives of social organizations in a demand for better legislation concerning honor crimes. My lawyer was there, along with other well-known figures. The government had been promising for a long time to outlaw crimes of honor but has done nothing. They should at least declare illegal all trials held before tribal councils, and change the laws that allow criminals to negotiate with the families of their victims and thus escape criminal sanctions. Some provincial governments are supposedly preparing legislation to regulate this system of private justice. The jirgas continue to wield power, however, and thousands of women are still the victims of rape or murder in this tribal system.

•   •   •

The appeals process, in my case, takes a long time. Two years have already passed since the initial death sentences. If the laws haven't changed, and the Supreme Court in Islamabad doesn't confirm the original verdicts, and the eight defendants who've already been released aren't penalized this time, as I requested in my appeal—then why not release everyone, and send me back to my village at the mercy of the Mastois? I don't dare think about it. Naseem is confident. She is at my side and completely committed to this combat. And I know that she's taking as many risks as I am. She's an optimist: she believes in my capacity to fight back. She knows that I'll go the distance, that I endure all threats with a fatalism that shields me, and a stubbornness that may seem placid to others, but which has been boiling inside me since the beginning.

I often say that if the justice of men doesn't punish those who did "that" to me, God will take care of it sooner or later. But I would like that justice to be given to me officially. In front of the entire world, if that's what it takes.

Dishonor

On March 1, 2005, I appear before a court once again. This time, it's the Lahore High Court Bench in Multan. I'm not alone: the NGOs and national and foreign presses await this verdict. I have announced to the many microphones waved in my direction that I hope only for justice, but that I want that justice to be "complete."

The Mastoi tribe is still denying everything. And all of us here know—NGO representatives, members of the local and foreign press—how regularly rapists are acquitted in our courts. The first verdict in my case was a victory, aside from the acquittal of the eight Mastoi men, whom I am still seeking to have punished. I sit there, listening to the judge read an interminable text in English, and of course I can't understand a single word.

"According to the verdict delivered by the antiterror-ism court of Dera Ghazi Khan on August 31, 2002, the six appellants named hereinbelow were judged guilty and sentenced to the following punish-ments. . . .

Six men were condemned to death.

The eight other prisoners were acquitted of all charges brought against them. . . ."

Naseem and I whisper together from time to time. And meanwhile, slowly but surely, as I listen to the rise and fall of those incomprehensible words, an arbitrary justice takes shape.

Tuesday passes like this, and so does Wednesday, March 2. Now it's my lawyer's turn to speak. I'm so tired that I doze off now and then. I often have the feeling that the proceedings in this large room are happen-ing without me.

If only I could understand what's being said! But I must wait for the evening, when my lawyer sums up for me the main arguments made by the defense, ac-cording to which it seems that . . .

My testimony "is full of contradictions, and not

supported by sufficient evidence to prove that a gang rape occurred."

Even though at least half the village was there to witness it.

"The complaint was not filed immediately after the events, and there was no reasonable explanation for this delay."

It takes a woman to understand how physically and psychologically damaged a woman is after being raped by four men. So, all these men would find it more logical if I'd committed suicide right away?

My testimony "was recorded in a questionable manner. A detective took down one version on June 30, 2002, which differs from the version given to the prosecutor."

My testimony could not agree with that submitted by the policeman, obviously.

There follows a whole series of denials put forward by the defense, all designed to show that nothing can prove the responsibility of the accused. This entire "story" has supposedly been invented by a reporter who happened to be around, in order to create sensational headlines. The press then pounced on the matter and gave it international coverage, when the alleged crime had never taken place!

I have received money from abroad—and I have a bank account!

I've heard all these arguments before, especially the last one. My desire to use that money to create a school for the education of girls—and even boys too—is of no interest to my adversaries. People have translated for me some of the commentary in the nation's newspapers arguing that Pakistan's women have but one duty, serving their husbands, and that a girl's only education should come from her mother, because aside from certain religious texts, there is nothing for her to learn. Except the silence of submission.

There seems to be an undercurrent of suspicion in this court that I am guilty of not observing this silence.

I have often said, and repeated to journalists, that I am fighting with the strength of my religious faith, with my respect for the Koran and the sunna, that heritage of Islamic custom based on the words and deeds of the Prophet. The form of tribal justice that consists of raping and terrorizing people to maintain control of a village has nothing to do with the Koran. My country, unfortunately, is still governed by barbarous traditions that the state has not managed to dislodge from people's minds. Judges can let themselves be swayed by their personal convictions when they choose between the official law of our Islamic republic, which is advancing too slowly toward true equality among the men and women of its citizenry, and the Islamic laws of *hudud*, which reinforce the strictures against *zina* and essentially penalize women.

On March 3, the verdict is finally delivered. Contrary to the decision reached by the antiterrorism court, and to general stupefaction, the Lahore High Court acquits five of the accused, ordering that they be released! Only one defendant remains in jail, condemned to life imprisonment. It's a devastating shock.

The crowd begins screaming in fury, refusing to leave the courtroom. The reporters twist and turn on the benches, everyone talking about what's happened.

"It's a sad day for the nation . . ."

"This is a disgrace for all women . . ."

"Once again, the law is just pushed aside . . ."

• • •

I'm thunderstruck. I'm shaking in front of the reporters. What can I say? What can I do? My lawyer
will appeal this decision, but in the meantime? "They"
will be going home, to their farm, a hundred yards
from my school and my home. My family is threatened, and I'm in mortal danger from this day on. I
wanted justice, I wanted them hanged—I wasn't
afraid to say so—or at least kept in prison for the rest of
their natural lives. I was fighting not only for myself,
but also for every woman scorned or abandoned by a
law that requires four male eyewitnesses to prove a
rape! As if rapists worked in public! All the testimony
that supports me has been thrown out, when *an entire
village* knows what happened. This court is trying to
restore their so-called lost honor to the Mastois by
adopting the defense's arguments, word for word, and
by turning me into the defendant: the investigation
was botched, the rape has not been proved. So, that's it,
Mukhtar, you had to be shut up, and the powerful Mastoi caste has beaten you. I'm being raped all over again.

It makes me weep with fury and anguish. Faced

with the general outrage, however, and the presence of demonstrators and journalists, the judge feels obliged to make a statement a few hours later.

"I delivered a verdict, but I have not yet ordered it implemented! The prisoners have not yet been released."

The verdict was announced on the evening of March 3, a Thursday. Friday is the day of prayer. So before the judge has time to have the verdict typed up and copies mailed to the prefect and various penal officials, we still have a few days in which to act, according to Naseem. She hasn't given up the fight, and neither have the activists from all the organizations who covered the trial.

Once the shock has passed, I refuse to give up. All around us, women are shouting with the same rage and humiliation. The NGOs and human rights organizations mobilize immediately: the province is in a ferment. On March 5, I hold a press conference, a grueling experience. Yes, I will appeal. No, I will not go into exile. I want to live in my home, in my village. This is my country, this land is my land, and I will appeal to President Musharraf himself if I have to!

The next day, I'm back at home, and on March 7, I

go to Multan to take part in a huge protest demonstration against this outrageous verdict. Three thousand
women are there, supported by women's rights organizations. I march surrounded by signs demanding justice in my name, and the reform of those infamous
hudud laws. I walk in silence amid this impassioned
throng as these humiliating words keep running
through my mind: "They're going to let them go,
they're going to let them go. . . . But when?"

Meanwhile, the organizers of the march take advantage of the microphones and photographers to further their protest.

"The government is still stuck in its own rhetoric
about women's rights," declares a militant spokesman
for a human rights organization. "Condemning Dr.
Shazia Khalid by forcing her to leave the country, and
Mukhtar Mai by freeing her assailants, means that we
still have a long road ahead of us before we attain justice."

The women who founded the AGHS Legal Aid Cell
have been fighting since 1980 for human rights and the
advancement of democracy in Pakistan, so they are fa-

miliar with difficult cases like mine. And they're even more bitter about the government's record. One of the founders, Hina Jilani, argues cases in the supreme courts in both Lahore and Islamabad.

"If the condition of women is improving a little, that doesn't have anything to do with the authorities. Any progress is due in large measure to civil society and to organizations supporting women's rights. Such people have often risked their lives to attain their goals! For years, we have been the targets of serious threats and constant pressure. This administration in particular uses the principle of women's rights to present a progressive and liberal image of the nation to the international community. It's all make-believe! The rape of Dr. Shazia Khalid and the verdict in Mukhtar Mai's case reveal this government's unwillingness to eliminate violence against women. The president protects the accused and influences criminal investigations. The state has lost its credibility."

"The condition of women has greatly deteriorated, and will keep growing worse," insists the director of the

Aurat Foundation, which focuses on education and legal aid for women. "We have a long way to go, even if human rights movements have made progress over the last quarter century. The government tells us that women make up 33 percent of the Parliament, but that is due entirely to constant pressure from civil society. The Mukhtar Mai verdict is a sure sign that nothing has been done to stop violence against women, and the rape of Dr. Shazia Khalid is an offense against human rights, another revolting example of the dishonor our nation has brought upon itself in the eyes of the world. The case of Mukhtar Mai can only encourage future rapists. The recent defeat of a proposed law against crimes of honor in this country means that we'll be marching—as we are doing today—for a long time yet before we can hope to achieve social justice."

Kamila Hayat, of the Human Rights Commission of Pakistan, also speaks to the press.

"Even if the violence has not diminished, women are now trying to understand what their rights are in situations of family violence, which are on the increase, as a result of poverty, a lack of education, and a host of other negative social factors, such as tribal judgments and the antifeminist laws in force for several years now. These two embattled heroines have shown us that any woman, whether she's educated or illiterate, will have to fight hard to obtain justice."

The press, the radio and television stations—all are busily discussing this scandalous verdict nonstop. Some commentators are asking themselves, who intervened in this? How can a judge completely reverse a conviction for premeditated gang rape handed down by an antiterrorism court? On what grounds? I don't have the answers. That's for my lawyer to figure out.

That very evening, I return to my village, because we have learned that Mrs. Margaret Huber, Canada's high commissioner in Pakistan, will be coming to visit me at the school the next day. The Canadian embassy, like all the foreign embassies, is aware of what has happened. Mrs. Huber will be arriving at around noon, and I'm anxious to give her a proper reception.

During her visit, she makes an announcement to the journalists accompanying her.

"Through the auspices of the Canadian International Development Agency, Canada will fund the expansion of the school to benefit the pupils already enrolled here and to accommodate those on the waiting list. My country is making this gift in recognition of the immense contribution of Mukhtar Mai, an activist in the struggle for equality between the sexes and for women's rights in Pakistan and throughout the world. Violence against women remains one of our greatest international plagues. What was done to Mukhtar Mai would have broken most other women. Gang-raped by order of a tribal council, Mukhtar Mai refused to remain silent, and with the funds she received in compensation, she built a school for her village. She has worked tirelessly to ensure that the girls of Meerwala will not suffer her fate. This woman embodies the true spirit of International Women's Day!"

Mrs. Huber spends four hours with us. Her presence is a comfort, but it's still a nerve-wracking day for me, spent hovering around the telephone, waiting for news from my lawyer, who is trying to obtain a copy of the verdict.

At last he learns that the "culprits" are to leave prison on March 14—in theory, because the media and the militants of the NGOs have posted themselves in front of the prison. The police can't guarantee the security of their charges in the face of this mob of furious demonstrators and reporters.

This scheduled release risks provoking a riot that the government really doesn't need. But since I've already been blamed for accepting help from the media and the NGOs, I'm not going to stay out of this. Far from it. It so happens that my fight is the same one they've been waging for years, and no one is going to make me keep silent. If I were to stay home and wail over my fate, I couldn't live with myself. I have responsibilities: the security of my family, my life, and my school, which now serves more than three hundred pupils.

God knows that I have always told the truth. And my courage is precisely that, the truth, and I want the truth to come out at last from that horrible hole where men hide with their hypocrisy. That's why Naseem and I undertake a week's tour that will leave us reeling from exhaustion.

On March 9, we prepare to leave the next day for Muzaffargarh, the county seat, where another demonstration to protest violence against women will take place. Around fifteen hundred people show up. The president of the Organization for the Defense of Human Rights in Pakistan makes a personal appearance to speak to the press. Huge posters bear the slogan COURAGE, MUKHTAR MAI—WE ARE WITH YOU!

We are escorted by the police everywhere we go. Sometimes I wonder if they are protecting me or keeping me under surveillance. I haven't been able to rest, I'm reeling with fatigue, and I've been shivering with a strange fever ever since March 3, the day the blow fell. Back in my village, some demonstrators have even camped out in front of my home: the path is crowded, and so is the courtyard. Those responsible for this gathering inform me that another demonstration, this time against the *hudud* laws, will take place in Muzaffargarh on March 16. I have no idea where I'll be on that date, however. The Mastois will be home again, free— but not me!

And it's off to Multan once more, to my lawyer's office, to pick up a copy of the court decision that he has just obtained. Another three hours on the road. I feel so sick . . . my head is like a stone, my legs are wobbly, my whole body is tired of fighting this endless battle. Naseem has to ask the driver to stop so that she can find some medicine to give me temporary relief.

Hardly have I entered my lawyer's office when my cell phone, a recently acquired safety measure, begins to ring. It's my brother Shakur, shouting hysterically.

"Come back to the house, quickly! The police have told us not to go out! The Mastois got out of prison an hour ago! They'll be arriving here soon and there are police all over the place! You have to get back here quickly, Mukhtar!"

This time, I seem to have lost the match. I'd hoped that the judicial authorities would intervene, and that my lawyer would have the time to file the appeal of this decision. I had hoped that something, anything, would happen, but that at least my assailants would remain in prison because of pressure from the media, the NGOs, and politicians. I'd been hoping for the impossible.

On our way home that night, I sense, I somehow know, that we're not far from the police van delivering the Mastois to their farm. They must be just ahead of us. . . . I stare at the rear lights of the vehicles up ahead and quiver with rage at the idea that we're stuck in back of them!

It's eleven at night when we get home. The house is surrounded by about ten police cars. And across the way, in the dense darkness, I can make out the same activity around the Mastoi farmhouse. They really are there! The police do not know whether the five men will try to escape during the appeal of the latest verdict, which is already under way. Above all, the police wish to avoid a disturbance and prevent any journalists or demonstrators from arriving. There are now guards at the entrance to the village, which is also its exit, since there is no other viable road.

"They can't leave home for the moment," Naseem reassures me. "Hurry up, get changed, we're leaving again!"

We've made the insane decision to drive to Multan: the lawyer has advised us to appeal directly to President Musharraf, and to ask him first of all to intervene for my safety and that of my family. But I want more. Much more. I want them all to go back to prison, I want the Supreme Court to reexamine the file. . . . I want justice! Even if it costs me my life. I'm not afraid of anything anymore. My anger is a wonderful weapon, and I am angry at this system that would like to force me to live in fear, in my own village, just down the path from the men who raped me and got away with it. The time is long gone when I trudged docilely up that path to beg pardon in the name of my family for the "honor" of those people.

They are the ones who dishonor my country.

After the three hours on the road to Multan, and eventually another nine hours on the bus to Islamabad, we arrive in the nation's capital on March 17, and in our wake come activists and reporters from all over. Concerned for my safety, I request a meeting with the minister of the interior, whom I ask to make certain that the Mastois will be forbidden to leave the territory. I know what they're capable of doing. Of assembling their clan, for example, and managing to slip into a tribal zone where no one would be able to identify them anymore. And of paying a cousin, an accomplice, to kill me. I imagine all their possible means of revenge: fire, acid, kidnapping. Burning down the house and the school.

When the minister receives us I am calm and firm, although utterly exhausted.

"You must understand that no one can bypass the judgment of the court in Lahore that easily."

"But I ask that you do something—my life is in danger!"

"There is a special procedure: in my capacity as minister of the interior, I can issue a new arrest warrant, in consideration of the fact that these men are a threat to public safety. But the state can exercise this option only during a period of seventy-two hours beginning at the moment of their release. That is the regulation."

Seventy-two hours. Three days . . . They arrived home on the evening of the fifteenth, and it's now the seventeenth. How many hours are left?

"I'm not familiar with the laws, Minister, or the regulations, but all I know is that the Mastois are on the loose and my family and I are in danger—I again request that you do something to protect us!"

The minister reassures me that he will do everything possible within his powers to ensure my safety, in accordance with the law.

. . .

We've been constantly on the go and I've only slept for two or three hours, but I give a press conference when I emerge from the office of the minister of the interior. Naseem and I can no longer tell the difference between day and night, and we can't remember the last time we ate.

At eleven o'clock the following morning, here we are in the office of the prime minister. We have counted up the hours more than ten times, and if our calculations are correct, the seventy-two hours ran out an hour ago.

The prime minister tries to reassure us too.

"We have taken care of it. I am sure that they were arrested before the seventy-two hours ran out. Trust me!"

"No. Personally, I would like a definite answer from you. Either I receive assurances that they are in prison, or I don't leave your office."

Naseem translates into Urdu, in the same resolute tone I used.

Who would ever have told me that I would speak

in that way to the prime minister of my own country? I, Mukhtaran Bibi, of Meerwala, a quiet, docile peasant woman, now called Mai, "respected older sister"— how I've changed! Here I am, sitting courteously but stubbornly in a lovely armchair in front of this official—and only the army could get me out of here before I've received confirmation that those savages have been sent back to prison. And I want to know exactly when that happened. If it has! Because, ever since March 3, I no longer trust anyone.

I am informed that the police received the new arrest warrant; a police escort has gone to get the Mastois in the village. At ten o'clock, the arresting officers handcuffed them, and the prefect is waiting. They will appear before him soon.

After leaving the prime minister's office, I call the prefect to check for myself, but he's in the neighboring district with all his colleagues: the president is visiting the area, and everyone is on duty. At least that visit has nothing to do with me. . . .

So I try to reach Shakur at our house, only to find that the call won't go through: we're in the middle of the rainy season, and it's impossible to speak to my brother. Finally, I manage to talk to a cousin who runs a shop.

"Yes, it's true! We saw the police this afternoon— they arrived right after Friday prayers to arrest all five of them, and even the eight others. And they have already taken them away. Oh, they were hopping mad! The whole village knows about it."

I should hope so.

I don't know what will happen next, so Naseem explains the legal procedures.

"The government of Punjab province has returned these men to prison through a special decision, but only for ninety days. The governor can have anyone he wants arrested simply by issuing an order, once he has decided that the person presents a threat to public safety. During this time, the court will be able to consider your appeal."

We return home on March 20, and the threats begin again. The Mastois' cousins are saying everywhere that they're going to do something against us, because it's our fault that the men were re-arrested. Now they are angry with Naseem, claiming that I wouldn't have been able to do anything without her. And that's true. We are friends, and we tell each other everything. We have faced things together, shared the same feelings of fear, anger, and joy. We have cried together, and fought back together. The fear is always there, waiting for us, but we have courage. During the press conference I gave after speaking with the minister of the interior, some reporters asked me if I wanted to leave Pakistan and seek asylum in another country. I replied that I had no intention of doing so and that I hoped to obtain justice here in my own homeland. And I emphasized that my school was operating successfully, with an enrollment of two hundred girls and a hundred and fifty boys.

That last statement was certainly true on March 16, but after March 20, things are quite different. Threatened once more with the loss of their gang leader, brothers, and friends, the Mastois seem to radiate fury and aggression for miles around. The police form a protective barrier around me, however, and although that may be cumbersome for my freedom of movement, I'm used to it.

On June 11, I learn that for my safety, I have been forbidden to travel. I had been invited to Canada and the United States by Amnesty International, but when I go to Islamabad to settle some formalities, I learn that I'm on something called the "exit control list," and am not permitted to leave the country.

And then my passport is taken away from me. Denied access to me, my lawyer angrily announces to the press that I am being held hostage somewhere in Islamabad, and that since I am his client, he absolutely must speak to me. The authorities inform him that as a security precaution, I'm under a form of house arrest. The president himself seems to feel that we must avoid "giving the nation a bad image abroad." These travel restrictions create a new stir among defenders of human rights and the international press.

During a debate in the Assembly, one senator—a woman—even declares that I have become "a Western woman" who should "show more modesty and discretion" by not traveling outside the country and by waiting instead "for the justice of God." Certain politicians are only too happy to openly reproach the NGOs for appealing to international lobbies. In short, it's in my "interest," as they put it, not to spread my story around the world, and to take care of everything here at home.

Claiming that I do not respect the laws of the Islamic Republic of Pakistan, certain extremists would like to force me to be quiet, but too many people support me, here in my country and abroad.

It's a long, hard road. . . . And then on June 15, I learn that the prime minister has instructed that my name be removed from the list of those forbidden to leave the country.

On June 28, there's a smile on my face. The Supreme Court of Islamabad has just agreed, after two days of hearings, to reopen my case. My lawyer, who had prudently asked me not to speak to journalists after I'd been put on the exit control list, is smiling as well.

"Now you can tell them whatever you want! No more restrictions from me!"

He had told reporters that as long as the Supreme Court had not yet decided to revisit the lower court's ruling, the support of the press might hurt my cause, since there should be no question about the independence of the Supreme Court. When I emerge from the last hearing, I face a barrage of questions. Overwhelmed with emotion, I embrace all the women who have helped me in my battle.

"I'm so happy, I feel really pleased. I hope that those who humiliated me will be punished. I will await the verdict of the Supreme Court, which will deliver justice here on earth."

And God's justice will come in its own time.

My lawyer confirms for the journalists that the eight other men who had previously been released, including the members of the village council who had premeditated the rape, are now in prison.

"This is not a case of simple rape, but a true act of terrorism. It was committed to spread terror throughout the village community. The decision to retry these men in the highest court of our land, so that all the evidence may be reexamined, is a most welcome development."

I was relieved. I could return to my village, my family, and my schoolchildren. The police surveillance lasted for a while longer—and was particularly noticeable whenever I agreed to an interview with foreign journalists. Afterward the pressure would subside, and the surveillance would be limited to an armed policeman guarding my door. But let a reporter from abroad show up at that door, and my "security" would appear.

There were still a few attacks here and there in the local press, and they weren't minor affairs. One of the most astonishing was an article about my request to travel outside the country, which created quite a controversy. I was still invited, in principle, to Canada and the United States, but I had publicly postponed those visits in order to allay any suspicions some people might have had. The truth is, I was not granted a visa. To keep me from giving Pakistan a bad name abroad! And what's more, people "in high places," as Naseem puts it, have claimed that all a woman has to do to become a millionaire and get a visa is . . . get herself raped. As if Pakistani women were going to rush through that "formality" to escape abroad! I deplore that indecent suggestion. Once more, the national and international press protested against such declarations.

It seems, however, that the statement in question might have been misinterpreted by reporters and didn't mean what it said. I hope so.

I have fought for myself and for all the women victimized by violence in my country. I have no intention of leaving my village, my house, my family, and my school. Neither do I have any desire to give Pakistan a bad name abroad. Quite the contrary: by defending my right to be a human being, by struggling against the principle of a tribal justice that sets itself up against the official laws of our Islamic republic, I'm convinced that I am supporting the political wishes of my country. No Pakistani man worthy of the name can encourage a village council to resolve a matter of honor by punishing a woman.

I have become, in spite of myself, a symbol for all those women who suffer the violence of patriarchs and tribal chiefs, and if this image of me has spread beyond our borders, it can only be a credit to my country. That is the true honor of my homeland: to allow a woman, educated or illiterate, to speak out in protest against an injustice done to her.

Because the real question my country must ask itself is, if the honor of men lies in women, why do men want to rape or kill that honor?

Kausar's Tears

Not a day goes by without women in a state of shock arriving here to seek help from me, and from Naseem as well. One day a journalist, a Pakistani woman, asked me how I was coping with that kind of celebrity in my homeland.

"Some women," I told her, "have assured me that if their husbands were to beat them, they wouldn't hesitate to threaten them right back: 'Watch out—I'll go complain to Mukhtar Mai!'"

It was a joke. But in real life, we deal with tragedy all the time.

On this day in October, while Naseem is helping me finish telling my story, two women arrive to interrupt me.

They've come from miles away to see me: a mother with her daughter, Kausar, a young wife of about twenty. Kausar carries her first child in her arms, a girl of perhaps two and a half, and tells us that she will soon give birth to a second baby. Her eyes are bright with fear, and tears streak her pretty face, pinched with fatigue.

"My husband quarreled with a neighbor, who used to come over to our house too often, to eat or sleep. My husband explained to him that we couldn't always receive him like that. One day, while I was preparing chapaties, four men burst into our house! One of them put a gun to my husband's forehead, another pointed his gun at my chest, and the other two wrapped a rag around my head—I couldn't see a thing. I could hear my husband's cries while they were dragging me along the ground, and I was afraid for the child I was carrying in my womb. They pushed me into a car, which drove for a long time, and when I heard a lot of traffic noise, I realized that they'd brought me to a city. They locked me inside a room, where for two months, they would come to rape me every day. I couldn't escape— the room was small, without any windows, and there were always several men guarding the door. I was a prisoner in that room from April to June. I used to think about my husband and child, fearing that they had died back in the village. I was going crazy, I would have liked to kill myself, but there was nothing in that room. They made me eat from a dish like a dog. And lap water like a dog. They took turns using me.

"And then, one day, they dragged me into a car again, with a cloth over my head, and once more drove for miles, out of the city. Then they threw me out into the road, sped away in the car, and left me there, all alone. I didn't even know where I was!

"I walked until I finally got back to my village, in the region of Muhammadpur, and I realized that the city where they'd taken me must have been Karachi, far to the south. When I got home, my husband was alive, my parents had taken care of my little girl, and they had filed a complaint with the district police. And I went myself to tell the police what had been done to me. I described the faces, I could recognize the four men, and my husband knew that the neighbor had become his enemy and taken his revenge on me. The police listened to me, and the officer had me sign a report with my thumb. Since I don't know how to read or write, he said that he would compose the report for me.

"But when the judge summoned me, and I told him everything that had happened to me, he said, 'You're not telling me the same thing that you told the police! Are you lying?'

"The judge summoned me twelve times, and each time I had to repeat that I didn't know what the policeman had written, but that I had told the truth. The judge had those four men brought in for questioning. They said that I had lied. They came to threaten my mother and father, insisting that they were not guilty, and that my parents had to tell that to the judge. When my father refused, they beat him and broke his nose.

"Finally, the judge put one of the men in prison, and let the three others go. We're so afraid of them! I don't know why just one of them is locked up—he wasn't the only one who raped me. Those men ruined my life and my family! I was two months pregnant when they raped me, my husband certainly knows this, but in the village, people are talking about me now. And those bad men are free! They're Baluch. They're more powerful than we are and despise my family, but we've never hurt anyone! My husband is my cousin, we've been married since childhood, and he's an honest man. When he went to the police, at first, no one listened to him. . . ."

Kausar cries silently, endlessly. I insist that she drink a little water, eat something, but she can hardly swallow. There's so much suffering in her eyes, and in her mother's, so much sad resignation. . . . Naseem will explain the law to them and tell them what association to apply to for a lawyer. We give them a little money to return to her village, but I know the road ahead will be long for her as well. If she has the courage to fight back, she and her family will live under constant threat until she receives justice. If she ever does. That family has no way of going elsewhere—their house, their lives are in that village. Her child will be born, and that tragedy will follow her to the end of her days. She will never forget. As I have not forgotten, either.

The law requires that the police draw up a preliminary investigative report. And it's always the same thing: they tell the woman, "Sign with your thumb, we'll write it down for you," and when this report reaches the judge, the culprits are always innocent, and the woman has lied!

A man wants to punish another for a village quarrel, so he organizes an armed kidnapping with the gang rape of an innocent young wife and mother, pregnant with her next child. The man is convinced from the beginning that he will go free, and even if he does go to prison, it's not for long. Sooner or later, he'll be released on appeal, for lack of "sufficient" proof. And people will probably say that the wretched woman consented, that she prostituted herself! Her reputation, her honor, and that of her family will be destroyed forever. And in the worst cases, she risks being condemned for adultery and prostitution, in accordance with the laws of *hudud*. To escape that monstrous punishment, either the accused would have to confess her "sin" before the judge, or the plaintiff would have to provide the famous four trustworthy eyewitnesses to the "sin."

Protected by such a system, criminals do as they please.

. . .

Another woman is waiting for me, her face half covered by a shabby veil. Worn out by housework, she has
no age. It's difficult for her to speak. She simply shows
me her face, discreetly, shamefully. And I understand.
Acid has eaten half of it away. And she can't even cry
anymore. Who did this? Her husband. Why? He used
to beat her, she wasn't serving him fast enough to suit
him. And now that he has mutilated her for life, he dis-
dains her. We can't do much for her—a little sympathy,
and some money so that she can leave her husband and
return to her own family, if she can.

Sometimes, the magnitude of the problem overwhelms
me. Sometimes I'm so angry I can hardly breathe. But I
never despair. My life has a meaning. My misfortune
has become useful to the community.

Educating little girls is rather easy, whereas boys,
who are born into this world of brutes and learn from
their elders' behavior, present a more difficult chal-
lenge. The justice dispensed to women must educate

them with each passing generation, since suffering and tears teach them nothing.

I await as well a definitive verdict from the Supreme Court. I trust in its justice here on earth as I trust in God for the last judgment. And if I were not to receive justice, if remaining in this village were to force me to endure endless war, and even one day to pay with my life, the guilty would be divinely chastised.

This October day draws to a close, with its share of pain and distress, but the dawn of the next day reveals other suffering. The earth has quaked all across the north of the country. There are thousands of dead and wounded, thousands of people homeless, thousands of famished children wandering in the ruins of what had been their lives. My province of Punjab escapes the catastrophe, and I pray for all those unhappy people, all those children lying dead in the wreckage of their schools.

Praying for them will not be enough. Pakistan needs international aid. This time, I am authorized to go abroad, with Dr. Amna Buttar, president of the Asian-American Network Against Abuse of Human Rights. A magazine has just named me its "Woman of the Year." I'm honored, of course, but that isn't the main reason for my trip.

I want to take advantage of this opportunity to plead the cause not only of women, but also, in these cruel times, of the victims of disaster. My heart truly bleeds for the women and children whose lives have been crushed, for those survivors who need help to stay alive.

So I take the plane to New York, after which I'll address the American Congress, in Washington, to plead these two causes and ask for fifty million dollars in additional aid to deal with the most deadly earthquake to have struck my country in many years.

The international aid is slow in coming. My country's image, unfortunately, does not elicit a flood of foreign charity. As usual, reporters follow me around, and some of their questions concern the possibility of my future exile. I have a simple response to such queries when I travel.

"My visit abroad will be short, and I will return to my country and my village as soon as possible."

True, I was named Woman of the Year by an American magazine that has previously honored some famous people, and I'm both pleased and touched by this recognition, but I was born Pakistani and will remain so. And I am traveling as a militant Pakistani woman, to help seek relief for my country, stricken by great misfortune.

If, through my strange destiny, I can thus bring help to my country and its government, it will be a great honor for us. May God protect my mission.

Mukhtar Mai
November 2005

Acknowledgments

I would like to thank:

My friend Naseem Akhtar for her faithful support;

Mustafa Baloch and Saif Khan, who agreed to be my interpreters during the writing of this book;

CIDA, the Canadian International Development Agency;

Amnesty International;

The International Association of Human Rights;

Dr. Amna Buttar, president of ANAA, the Asian-American Network Against Abuse of Human Rights;

And all the organizations in defense of women's rights in Pakistan, and the women activists combating violence against women throughout the world, who stood by me in my own struggle;

And all the donors, both official and private, who

funded the construction of the Mukhtar Mai School and its expansion.

Finally, I thank most particularly my little pupils, girls and boys, whose hard work at the school inspires me to hope that in my village, I will see the growth of a better-educated generation, in which men and women are free and at peace with one another.

If you would like to make a donation,

or to find out more about

Mukhtar Mai and her schools,

please contact the Mukhtar Mai

Women Welfare Organization at

www.mukhtarmaiwwo.org.

IN THE NAME OF HONOR

Mukhtar Mai

with Marie-Thérèse Cuny
translated by Linda Coverdale

A Readers Group Guide

About this Guide

The suggested questions are intended to help your reading group find new and interesting angles and topics for discussion for Mukhtar Mai's *In the Name of Honor*. We hope that these ideas will enrigh your conversation and increase your enjoyment of the book.

Many fine books from Washington Square Press feature Reader's Club Guides. For a complete listing, or to read the guides online, visit www.BookClubReader.com.

Questions for Discussion

1. Mai describes her shifting thoughts after the rape, from numb devastation and plans for suicide to determination for justice. What were the personal and cultural factors that led to her suicidal thoughts? What pulled her out of them? In what ways did Mai's experience take away her fear of the consequences of speaking out?

2. Throughout her account, Mai speaks passionately about the power that literacy holds. Is education something we take for granted in our culture? How could Mai's story have been different if she had been literate? In what ways is knowledge power?

3. Mai writes that at the time of her initial police interviews, she knew "*absolutely nothing about the official justice reserved for wealthy and educated people*." (pg. 29) Does her culture treat justice as a right or a privilege? How does this differ from the mind-set in the United States? How is her assumption of justice for the privileged complicated by the story of Dr. Shazia Khalid? (pg. 125)

4. In describing her divorce, Mai attributes her freedoms to "*stubbornness, the only weapon we women have against men*." (pg. 41) How did Mai use stubbornness to her advantage? Was this a characteristic she already held, or was it also fostered by her experience? How do you think the Western feminist movement was aided by women's "stubbornness"?

5. After the verdict is read in her trial, Mai says, "*I can return to my village with my head high, and modestly covered with the traditional shawl.*"(pg. 74) What does this statement tell us about Muslim feminism? Is it possible to have personal pride within cultural modesty?

6. What are the varied connotations of rape in Mai's society? How is the accusation used in relation to premarital sex and unwanted marriage? In what senses do those in power view sex as a threat? How does this relate to rape's use as a means of punishment?

7. *In the Name of Honor* describes Mukhtar Mai's two struggles, primarily against an oppressive society, but also against the limitations she had imposed upon herself. How

does her personality evolve throughout the narrative as she changes from Mukhtaran Bibi into Mukhtar Mai? What role does Naseem play in helping Mai become a more empowered individual?

8. Mai is accused of disloyalty to Pakistan because of her outspoken efforts to change her culture, yet she speaks passionately about her love for her home. Do you think Mai's advocacy proves or undermines her patriotism?

9. Mai comments that in her work with both girls and boys at her school, she has come to see that both genders are caught in the net of her society's attitudes towards women. In which ways are men enslaved by their culture? How does the school help to free them as well?

10. Pakistani activist Hina Jilani says, in relation to Mai's story, that "if the condition of women is improving a little, that doesn't have anything to do with the authorities. Any progress is due in large measure to civil society and to organizations supporting women's rights." (pg. 140) What is your opinion of personal advocacy and activism? Has Mai's story changed your viewpoint or reinforced it?

Reading Group Tips

* Find out more about the struggle for women's rights in Pakistan from an organization like Human Rights Watch. For information on how to help, visit hrw.org/campaigns/pakistan/index.htm or the Human Rights Commission of Pakistan's website: www.hrcp.cjb.net.

* For up to date information, as well as links to interviews and press coverage about Mukhtar Mai, visit en.wikipedia.org/wiki/Mukhtaran_Bibi.

* Violence against women is a global issue. To find out more visit www.4woman.gov/violence.

* Mukhtar Mai becomes an agent of change in her community through promoting reading and education. To find out what you can do in your community and about literacy, visit www.nifl.gov, www.theliteracysite.com, www.proliteracy.org, www.famlit.org, and www.rif.org.